Fun and Fulfilling Careers One Question at a Time

A Step-by-Step Guide to Thriving in Your

Personal and Professional Life

Heather H. Bennett

creative**brand**coach

Table of Contents

Forward by David J.P. Fisher

If I go far enough down my family tree, I am going to find someone who was a fisher. His dad had probably been a fisher, and his son would probably be a fisher. It would make sense that everyone would refer to him by the family profession: Fisher.

Luckily, things have changed. Now, you have freedom to divine and carve out your own career and your own path. No matter what your parents did for work, you get to decide what you will do for a living. And you get to decide how you will go about doing it and even the "why" that motivates you.

That freedom comes with embedded responsibility. Since you can choose what to do with your life, you also *have to choose* what to do with it. Uncovering your career path is a dynamic process that requires you to fully engage.

And for that kind of path, it helps to have a map.

That is why I love *Fun and Fulfilling Careers One Question at a Time*. It's not a color-by-numbers book, it's a blueprint. And it's the blueprint for whatever you want to build in your professional world. Heather takes you through the process that she has painstakingly crafted to work with her clients over the years. And she maps out exactly how you can define the work you want to do and, just as importantly, communicate that clearly to your network, your partners, and your potential clients.

I have spent over 15 years coaching and consulting with thousands of small business owners, entrepreneurs, and sales professionals on how to build their businesses and create better outcomes. That could mean anything from bringing in more clients, to developing a stronger online presence, to growing a start-up. My books, like **Networking in the 21st Century: Why Your Network Sucks and What to Do About It** and **Hyper-Connected Selling** have been read around the world.

Over that time, I've found that one of the critical pieces of long-term professional success is self-awareness. It's incredibly powerful when someone knows why they do the work they do, how to most effectively serve their customers, and how to communicate that to everyone they meet.

And from the first time Heather and I sat down for a conversation, I knew that she understood that power inside and out.

Her own brand and skills are as wonderfully wrapped up in her personal story as you think they would be. She draws on a solid foundation built from helping large, well-known brands define and communicate their messages. She combines the analytic skills of an MBA with the empathy skills she developed raising 4 awesome kids. And she has been building her own business (and taking her own medicine) for years.

Which is why sitting down to get her feedback on how you can grow your business and your brand creates such a huge impact on people's careers.

And you might not be able to sit down with her across a café table or Zoom call. But you'll find everything you need in here to accelerate your career... and enjoy the process while you are doing it.

David J.P. Fisher

Author of **Networking in the 21st Century** series and **Hyper-Connected Selling**

Introduction

Why I Wrote This Book

Twenty years ago, I was approached by a friend from grad school. Her sister, "Emily," was trying to decide what to do with her career. Emily was a successful graphic designer, but she was disillusioned with how her career would progress within the agencies that employed graphic artists. She could not see how the expected path would make her happy.

Should she stay where she was or create a new business?

This was not a small, quick, or easy question for her to answer.

At the time, I was working in brand management for a consumer products company. Brands were then, and still are, my passion. So why would my friend's sister need my help? I was not in human resources or life coaching or anything remotely involved in career decision-making. At the time, I was just a newly minted MBA, a businessperson that was great at analyzing data, making decisions, and creating strategies to get goals achieved.

Four cross-country telephone calls later, my first personal branding client had her answer: start her own graphics design company. She is still happily working today as the founder and president of that graphics design company with great fulfillment.

Fast forward ten years and many small business and start-up clients later. At this time, I thought I was focusing on solving business problems… and I did help owners and founders with their business problems. What became more apparent with each client was the consistent methodology with which I was helping them. It always started with their brand, not the products or services they were selling—who they were at their core as a founder, salesperson, venture capitalist, entrepreneur, owner, educator, artist, professional....

By focusing on who they were at their authentic core, I was first able to understand the motivations behind their business decisions. By figuring out what they were good at, what they were passionate about, and what goals they needed to achieve to feel and be successful, I was able to help them form a plan to satisfy all of these and often more.

It seemed a lot like life or career-coaching to help people achieve their personal best. My unique spin on how I helped them was understanding their personal brand.

Five years go by and I decided to get my methodology down on paper. Another client offered me the perfect opportunity to test out a formalized process. She was looking to create a consistent brand across a wide span of businesses she worked in including consulting, writing, guest appearances on radio and TV, her online persona, and podcasts. Aha! An actual personal branding strategy project.

The concept of personal branding was now established in the business world. Books and articles on it were all over Amazon, magazines, and social media. I was thrilled! Finally, what I was doing for my clients had a real, recognized name. And I soon learned the way that I helped my clients create their personal brand was unique even in the realm of personal branding experts.

Discovering My Unique Method of Personal Branding

My unique personal branding method focuses on the consistency of a person's brand over long periods of time to find the most authentic expression of their unique personal brand. I look for the handful of words that describes the personal brand of that unique individual. A short-list of characteristics that, when viewed against the path of a person's life and career, explained how they moved from one role to the next. These are the touchstone characteristics that explained why they gravitated towards certain work or were more successful at one type of work rather than another.

By examining their lives from early childhood through their education and experiences, we are able to see patterns of behavior, characteristics, and decision-making that created the core of their brand. The patterns demonstrated what will likely occur in their future career and life. More importantly, the patterns showed where changes in habit or knowledge could allow for a smoother transition into a new lifestyle or career.

Understanding where opportunities to affect or change the future are the key to increasing your success and enjoyment when choosing how to spend your time.

My personal branding method encourages choices that bring fulfillment and joy for the individual. Once people find a higher level of fulfillment in their work and lives, they are more able to look beyond themselves.

The oxygen mask analogy from airplane flights where passengers are encouraged to put on their own oxygen mask first before helping others applies here. You cannot help others without first taking care of your basic needs. The concept can be pushed even further to say that helping others will result in more successful outcomes only when the helper has first satisfied their own unfulfilled needs.

By helping individuals find and live their unique personal brand – basically helping them put on their own oxygen mask first – I give them the time, opportunity, and motivation to make the world a better place.

I honed my methodology over several years. While helping one brand client in the media industry, I began reading tons of books/blogs/social media posts on coaching, self-help, business excellence, leadership, etc. As I spent time writing down the method to present to this client on how to fix her business issues, the words began to take shape as a series of questions, real-life examples and research. When I was laid up recovering from an aggressive knee surgery for an old sports injury, I distracted myself by studying social media through an online certificate program of six courses and a capstone project via Northwestern University Medill School. Through the program, I gained an invaluable understanding of how social media platforms can be used to create and reinforce a personal brand.

I tested my methodology in a group session when another colleague, Amy, needed help designing and hosting a retreat. With the help of some amazing people - whom I thank in the acknowledgments - I created my **Personal**

Branding for Fulfillment in Life, Work & Play workbook as a guide to my personal branding methodology. I've since used the workbook at a retreat, in one-on-one consulting, and relied on it when presenting at my workshops. Some people found new careers, some people recognized that they really were in the right job all along, some people took intentional time to step back from the frantic pace of their lives or pushed forward in new ways with success and happiness...I was helping people. Yeah!

The feedback from the retreat and workshops was that what really made the workbook amazing was what I was saying to them while walking them through the workbook. It really needed a little more explaining than what was in the workbook. Without me to guide them through the workbook, it was difficult, sometime confusing, and certainly not fun. And that is why I wrote this book. In this book I gently walk you through my process of personal branding, making it as enjoyable as possible and, most importantly, leaving you with the practical tools and a concrete plan to get you where you want to go.

Organization of This Book

The purpose of this book is to help you create your personal brand so it reflects who you are, what you bring with you, where you are needed, and how you will get where you want to go.

Chapters 1, 2, and 3 examine your authentic personal brand and work experiences. These exercises will guide you to discover your unique talents, skills, and personality traits – basically who you are at your core, your authentic self in the context of your past and present work, hobbies, commitments and volunteer work.

Chapter 4 helps you look back at your experiences to recognize the type of work and activities that truly bring you fulfillment. The chapter exercises highlight which experiences best utilize your skills and talents. By examining which activities you have chosen or avoided, you will better understand which activities in the future will match with your personal brand and give you the most joy and fulfillment.

The exercises in the first four chapters help you create your personal brand statement. The personal brand statement acts as a mission statement to keep your future in line with your goals. By the end of these exercises, you will have a written description of your personal brand, and a list of the activities that best use your time, talent, and energy to make your life more fulfilling!

Chapter 5 inspires you to describe your ideal future. By listing the environment and circumstances that would best fit your personal brand, you are able to recognize when those opportunities are presented to you.

Chapter 6 teaches you how to research where a need exists in the world for your unique skills and talents. This need could be a job position, new product development, startup company, non-profit organization, or something completely different. By showing you how to research and think outside of the box, the exercises will open the door to even more opportunities.

Chapters 7 and 8 help you plan to reach your professional goals using your personal brand statement. These are the goals designed to bring you fulfillment. These goals could be a new career, new role in your current company, change in the priorities of your personal life or a reorganization of how you spend your time. For every person, this is a unique and different journey.

Finally, within each chapter, topics are discussed to help with the everyday management of life, career, and your personal brand. Topics include recommendations about career management, motivation, organization, and productivity that emphasize certain points or explain the purpose of a specific exercise.

At the end of the book, I have listed some resources to help as well.

How to Read This Book

Each section of the book starts by discussing the concepts that help you get through each step with background research, case studies, and stories that highlight examples of how each concept makes your personal brand better, one question at a time.

Next, easy to follow exercises help you work through that chapter's concepts. Use a notebook, journal, composition book or electronic file to have a single, easy to review and store working document with lots of space for writing in your answers to the personal branding questions.

Exercises and homework assignments are used throughout to create an active learning structure that will help you absorb more of the information you are learning… in this case what you are learning about yourself. In talking about how we learn, studies by Kelly Hogan proved that active learning raised test scores by 3%. Active learning in this situation was described as including pre-class preparatory homework and in class activities.

By having you work on exercises throughout, you will most likely retain more of the knowledge you gain about yourself and what your future work and personal life could look like. It is worth your time and effort to try to do as many exercises as you can.

> *"What you put into life is what you get out of it." – Clint Eastwood*

Three Simple Steps for Using This Book:

1. Read the paragraphs at the beginning of each chapter

2. Do the exercises and answer questions in a notebook, journal, or electronic document.

3. Take notes on what you want to remember most from each section

The purpose of this book is to give you the tools and plans to get you to the life you want. Let's get started!

Part One: **Discovering and Building Your Personal Brand**

How to Plan and Prepare for Your Next Career or New Challenge with Passion, Authenticity, and Hope

What determines when we decide to change our lives? Our careers? What do we need to do to create the lives we want? How do we get the jobs that will fulfill us? How well do we really know what we want? And then, is what we want going to get us to the life we need?

> *"Between stimulus and response there is a space. In that space is our power to choose our response. In our response lies our growth and our freedom."*
> *– Viktor E. Frankl*

The ideal answer to a string of questions can sometimes be found in an animated film song. "You've got to dig a little deeper." Wise words from the wise Mama Odie in Disney's *The Princess and the Frog*. Besides being a lovely nod to the wonderful treasures of New Orleans that keep me traveling there, the film follows the stories of a multitude of characters that think they know what they need, but clearly are focused on what they don't. So how can we "dig a little deeper"?

Part of digging deeper is doing the hard work of peeling back the layers of decoration and armor we pile on just to get through each day. To get to know ourselves better, we need to remove the distracting accessories and look at

9

what is underneath. The world, our employers, our customers, families, and friends require us to do the job we promised to do. We need to live up to their expectations. So, we cover up our authentic selves with the uniform or costume necessary to look the part.

In this process, we can lose sight of our authentic selves and forget the passion behind our choices on how to spend our time working, playing, volunteering, and living. Losing sight of our true passionate selves decreases the joy and sense of fulfillment doing these activities. Over time this decrease in authenticity leads to lower success rates and a lessened performance quality. It also prevents us from filling our customers' or clients' needs. This lowered success rate then causes us to give up—a self-fulfilling prophecy.

What if you could choose?

What if you could craft and design a life that encouraged you to dive in and be more fully a part of what makes life worth living? Why not choose a career or activity that makes you feel happy and alive? The only real question is: how to accomplish this?

How do you find a fulfilling career?

By finding your true authentic self. By allowing yourself the luxury of dreaming about finding a career and work you love.

Find your authentic self.

Discover work and activities that bring you joy and use your skills, talents, and experience best.

Build a personal brand that helps to do that work.

*"If you don't like the road you're walking,
pave another one." – Dolly Parton*

The purpose of this book is to help you choose the life you need to be your best. And help you understand why the life you need can become the life you want and the life you love. The distinction being what we want is not always what we need. But eventually what we need will lead us to what we love.

Another delightful person that embraces the importance of giving is Meghan Murphy. I met Meghan while travelling on the East Coast and have been continuously astounded by how one small story of her walking on the beach transformed into a global movement to spread kindness.

Meghan is the creator, founder, and Chief Officer of Kindness for The Kindness Rock Project. Her story goes that she found a rock that gave her hope when she needed it the most, simply by being there. She decorated a rock with an uplifting message and then left it on the beach for someone else to find when they needed it. Later, it was picked up by a friend who told Meghan about how it helped the friend when she really needed some encouragement. Meghan tried to keep her secret to herself, but a news team found out about the rocks she had continued to decorate and let her secret out.

Instead of shying away from the attention, Meghan chose to step into the spotlight to help others and share the stories that inspire versions of The Kindness Rock Project.

Schools, church congregations, military companies, neighborhoods, book groups, camps, retreats, corporations and more have used The Kindness Rock Project to create more joy, love, and kindness in a world that so desperately needs it. Thank you, Meghan, and The Kindness Rock Project team for knowing how one small act can inspire greatness in all of us.

The joy of giving without needing anything in return.

The karma of hoping for the best and yet not ever expecting it.

My hope is to encourage you to choose your career path by making it doable through easy to follow steps, and fun narratives to keep you motivated. The planning and changing of your future should bring you joy and be a fun process.

Chapter 1 Personal Branding Basics

What is Personal Branding?

Personal Branding is the skills, talents, personality traits and passions of an individual that are consistently communicated through all interactions with others, online and offline. Your personal brand is designed to create a life in sync with your authentic self.

After spending years developing strong brands for small businesses, non-profits, professionals, and startups (particularly the founders), I discovered that simultaneously developing each founder's personal brand would increase the success rate of the new venture. After all, the founder is usually the face and driving force of the business.

One example is the president of a small consumer product company, who I'll call "Mike." Mike had a unique story that pulled from the emotional depths of his life to create a product he could not stop himself from producing. For most consumer products, placement is a key business issue and problem. Your product must be in front of the consumer or there is no chance it will get sold. Negotiating placement in large, national stores for a small start-up is almost impossible. However, Mike's story and reason for creating the product was so compelling that he has - and continues to get - shelf space in the most unlikely of places without a huge company behind him. All of this is because of the strength of his personal brand. The story of Mike's life is the compelling reason the product gets shelf space and has created a loyal following.

Why Should I Create a Personal Brand?

With every interaction we have with people around us, we leave an impression. Whether that impression accurately reflects who we really are and what we want to communicate depends on how cognizant we are of the delivery. How we deliver the message, what we say and to whom we say it, can alter the anticipated result. Your personal brand is a guide to make sure you are intentionally communicating what you want others to understand about you and your message.

Working with small businesses and start-ups is wonderfully exciting and terrifyingly risky. Passion and drive fuel the founders and early employees. Breaking into a new market or even creating one can be life-changing at the deepest level and the commitment and dedication to the mission of the fledgling company needs to be strong and dependable. Over the last few decades, many of my clients fell into the business category of start-ups.

The most successful of these businesses were the ones where the founder had a clear and authentic personal brand. An authentic personal brand allows you to focus on what business activities will give you fulfillment through meeting a need in the world. It allows your business to provide the product or service that it uniquely can offer to the ideal customer. By identifying their personal brand, my clients and I were able to lay out a strategy that matched their personal brand to the marketing needs of their business. From these success stories and plenty of experimentation, I developed a method to improve the fulfillment of my clients and the success of their business through a better understanding of their own unique personal brand.

The question is not whether you have a personal brand, because you already do.

The actual question is whether you understand, manage, and communicate your personal brand in a way that leads to success and helps you reach your goals.

> *"We all have personal brands and most of us have already left a digital footprint, whether we like it or not. Proper social media use highlights your strengths that may not shine through in an interview or application and gives the world a broader view of who you are. Use it wisely." - Amy Jo Martin, Celebrity Brand Strategist to Shaquille O'Neal, Dana White (UFC) & Dwayne "The Rock" Johnson*

In the example above, my client's story was the compelling ingredient that brought life to his product. Over the years, he stayed true to his story and made sure the product, packaging and marketing reflected his authentic personal brand.

However, a few years after working with me, he hired a mid-tier marketing firm to grow his business. They changed the look, feel and marketing message of the brand to move farther away from who he is as the founder. By taking his personal brand out of the mix, the product sales and placement in stores plummeted. The firm did not take the time to get to know his story. The marketing firm never considered how important the personal brand of the founder was to the health of the business.

The reasons for creating a strong personal brand are many: business goals, growth, and financial health are just a few. Consistency and respect for your customer is another.

I am happy to report that since that experience, with my renewed guidance he redirected his marketing back to reflecting his personal brand and sales and distribution are improving.

Just consider what a strong personal brand could do for you.

How to Build a Personal Brand
Building a personal brand consists of the following building blocks: self-awareness, experience, opportunity, and a strategic plan.

Self-awareness is found through understanding the skills, personality traits, and talents that make up who you are at your core.

Experience is the combination of work, volunteer roles, and commitments that control and guide how you have spent and continue to spend your time.

Opportunity occurs after a combination of the research, expert interviews, and ideal job posts has been completed guiding you towards a future career or role.

The *strategic plan* lists the actions needed to fully utilize your personal brand through networking and connecting, continuous learning and maintaining your personal brand.

The exercise at the end of the chapter will start you on your path for creating your personal brand. But first, let's get you in the right mindset.

The diagram below shows how these discovery points are the building blocks of your personal brand.

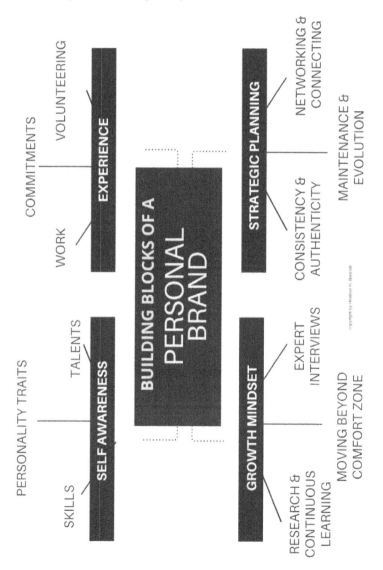

Planning is More than Half the Fun

Working on your personal brand to achieve your goals requires a lot of planning. The importance of the planning process should not be overlooked. Besides providing a guideline for how to achieve a goal, the act of planning has benefits as well.

In the *7 Hidden Benefits of Planning*, Erin Condren, Chief Creative Officer of Erin Condren Designs LLC, states "Actively planning, instead of passively reacting, is proven to reduce stress and can lead to more fulfilling, intentional living." The article also includes citations from psychologist Robert Epstein and cognitive neuroscientist Stanislas Dehaene about how planning decreases stress and improves memory, especially when writing the information on paper.

Discovering the benefits of mindfully completing the exercises in this book was inspiring. While researching the benefits from the action of planning, I noticed multiple research studies and articles exploring other types of planning from vacation planning to hobbies.

As fun as a spontaneous last-minute vacation can be, studies have shown that the planning of a vacation adds to the effectiveness of it to recharge our spirits and restore our energy. Below are a few quotes about the importance of planning in the overall benefit of a vacation or event. Which of these quotes on planning resonate the most with you? Write that quote down and use it as motivation when you plan your next vacation or activity.

"It's statistically proven that time spent planning vacation directly correlates with greater happiness in your personal and professional lives." – Amanda Mulligan of Travelzoo

Travel writer, Annie Daly of SELF magazine, lists her plan for prioritizing travel, "When you're traveling, you're forced to deal with new experiences and stimuli at a faster pace, which means that, if you handle them well, you may end up experiencing more 'small feelings of success' than you do at home."

Psychologist Michael Brein, Ph.D., host of The Travel Psychologist Travel Tales audiobook series, said, "Those successes are so rewarding that many people return from trips feeling a lot better about themselves, like they've achieved—which leads to higher self-esteem overall."

"The practical lesson for an individual is that you derive most of your happiness from anticipating the holiday trip," Jeroen Nawijn, a researcher studying holidays.

"Turns out, there is an art to anticipation." said Elizabeth Dunn, an associate professor of psychology at the University of British Columbia and a leading happiness researcher, "Savoring is an active, not passive, process."

"It's better to immerse yourself," suggests Prof. Dunn. "Reading novels and poetry, watching films and television programs, browsing fashion and design blogs that are either from or about the place you plan to visit encourages you to not only learn about your destination, but to dream, providing some concrete details for your mind to latch on to. It may sound counterintuitive, but this building up of positive expectations and excitement actually helps our minds smooth over any minor discrepancies if reality doesn't quite measure up to the fantasy" – Stephanie Rosenbloom, *The New York Times*.

If the activity of planning can increase your happiness, then it seems advantageous to be mindful as you plan and reap the benefits during the actual process.

A final example of how the action of planning improves our mental and emotional state is preparing for leisure activities such as hobbies.

Planning (or the methodical action of preparing for an activity) is part of what makes hobbies rewarding. Whether that is spending hours researching the perfect set of golf clubs online or walking the floor of a comic book convention or carefully chopping and mincing the ingredients for a masterpiece of a meal.

Do not take this preparation lightly as it will help you gain further fulfillment from your life and career. And if you see a pattern in what part of planning you enjoy; you may find a new hobby that brings you fulfillment.

Self-Care for the Future

Practicing and scheduling self-care is important to prepare for the unpredictable. Self-care is one way to make sure when your plans are derailed and emergencies occur, you will have the fortitude to handle the unknown without wasting time.

By creating self-care routines and habits, you are better able to focus on your personal brand, career and goals. A strong self-care regime gives you the reserves needed to protect your livelihood and dreams when the unexpected inevitably occurs.

What is self-care?

This definition from a psychcentral.com post explains: "Self-care is any activity that we do deliberately in order to take care of our mental, emotional, and physical health." – Raphailia Michael, MA.

> *"Those who think they have not time for bodily exercise will sooner or later have to find time for illness." – Edward Stanley*

My short list of self-care habits includes:

- Plan and take vacations.
- Schedule medical checkups and follow the directions of your practitioners to keep you healthy.
- Workout and do post workout relaxation like a long shower, spa, or sauna.
- Meditate through mindfulness and breathing.
- Do at least one thing a day that makes you laugh and smile.
- Be grateful.
- Connect with others.

"It's the heightened state of being that lets whatever you're doing be your best life, from moment to astonishing moment."
– Oprah Winfrey

If you need more concrete directions for adding self-care into your schedule, see the articles cited in the notes section at the end of this book or the joy creator and time management topics in Chapter 4.

The Gift of Journaling

Discovering your personal brand requires intense self-awareness. One tool to help with self-awareness is journaling. Journaling is a gift to yourself. Years or even months from now, looking back on what was most important or top of mind at the time gives your perspective on how you handle life, set and reach goals as well as how to improve where you are currently.

A great benefit of journaling is that it helps us better understand the reoccurring bad habits or roadblocks that each of us puts up for ourselves—sometime unintentionally and without being aware. These roadblocks and bad habits can consistently keep you from feeling you have achieved or moved forward in life. They can prevent you from achieving goals and growing as a person. They can mislead you to remove the key team member or people in your life than can help you find success.

A little effort can lead to lasting results when it comes to journaling. Stop procrastinating and start tonight writing just one sentence about what you most remember about your day. The one sentence journal is a Gretchen Rubin creation that makes even the busiest of us able to keep track of what was most important to us that day.

The key to successful journaling is finding a method that works for you and your lifestyle. Even a regular series of emails back and forth to a sibling, spouse, or college roommate can become a form of a journal. Be openminded about the options that work within your schedule and the energy you can bring to a journal consistently.

In a few weeks, look back at your entries and see what concerns or successes keep coming up. Those repetitive themes offer the opportunity to make changes in your life by working around them or solving them. You also might see a pattern of what brings you happiness and joy. Consider cutting out your favorite one sentence journal notes and carrying them around like fortunes from fortune cookies to inspire you.

Finding Hope to Reach Your Goals

Hope is the reason we can achieve great things and overcome obstacles. It is also the reason we move forward in life.

Trying to figure out what to do with your life or career can be daunting and overwhelming. Consciously being hopeful will help you push away the hesitations and self-doubt that can interrupt the process of building your dreams with your personal brand.

"Hope does not disappoint"
– Romans 5

In the book *Out of the Maze* by Dr. Spencer Johnson, MD, the main character is stuck without being able to move beyond their own limited view of the world... our maze. The author discusses how we can better handle change which is inevitable. The main character ventures off finally to do something about the change around him and encounters a new character, which we later find out is Hope. Hope patiently waits for the realization that changes his thinking.

"'I don't think things ever go back to how they were," said Hope. "Here's my thought, though: maybe they can turn out better than they were.'"

Out of the Maze is the sequel to *Who Moved my Cheese?*, also by Dr. Johnson. The books are short, easy to read and in combination tell an extended parable that breaks through the assumptions that hold back business and personal growth. The books give specific strategies to get around those assumptions towards a more successful, happy, and growth minded existence.

In this book, I want to help you find hope by remembering what inspired you in the past and find what will inspire you in the future. True understanding of yourself and your personal brand requires a lot of energy and drive.

"Optimism is the faith that leads to achievement. Nothing can be done without hope and confidence." – Helen Keller

Hope and inspiration work together to give you that extra push to move forward in your life. The topics in this chapter (and every chapter) are written to inspire hope, give you motivation, and keep driving you towards your goal.

Chapter 1 Exercises

Goals and Reasons

Congratulations! You have reached the first exercise.

This first exercise may be the most important one. It is designed to give you a guide and the motivation to go through and successfully complete all the other exercises and make it more fun and exciting in the process.

> *"Don't let perfectionism become an excuse*
> *for never getting started."*
> *– Marilu Henner*

For this exercise, write down why you are reading this book. Not why you think you should read this book but, for you personally, why are *you* reading this book? Be specific and detailed. Why did you pick up this book?

It sounds like a simple question, but is it? Here are some questions that may help you answer the question (use these questions as a starting point for inspiration rather than a check list to answer):

What do you hope the book will do for you?

What are you hoping to achieve?

What is missing in your life?

What is the reason behind you needing a change in your life?

What has changed about you or the world around you that compels you to want more or need more out of life?

What about your life seems disconnected or out of tune?

What do you love or not love about your career or situation?

What challenges in your life do you want to resolve?

What challenges do you feel this book may clarify and help you overcome?

Your answer to why are you reading this book is incredibly important for you and for me as well. I wrote this book with the intention of making the world a better place through helping people find fulfillment by taking charge of their lives.

"The only impossible journey is the one you never begin." – Tony Robbins

Understanding why you want a change is important for you to get the most out of reading this book and doing the exercises and the thinking required to make that happen.

Think about and write down what goal or goals you hope to achieve during your time focusing on your unique and authentic personal brand.

Note: you do not need to read the whole book or even complete all the exercises at one time. I designed this book, the exercises, and topics so that you could choose the ones that most resonate with you, your needs, and your current situation. It is a tool to help you achieve your goals.

"I choose to make the rest of my life the best of my life." – Louise Hay

Choose a goal that you can note and celebrate to acknowledge that you have grown as a person. Use the SMART method to create a goal that is Specific, Measurable, Achievable, Relevant and Timely.

How to Set

S.M.A.R.T.
GOALS

S = Specific

M=Measurable

A = Achievable

R = Relevant

T = Timely

Image designed by Heather H. Bennett

Even wanting to know yourself better is a great goal. In our busy hectic lives, self-awareness can be difficult to achieve.

What event, action, or achievement must happen so that you feel you have truly made the effort?

Write it down.

Keep it where you can read it during the time you are going through this book. Use a journal, notebook, or a file on your favorite electronic device to keep track of your progress. Write/print out your goals on a bookmark, so you can keep them squarely in front of you during the time you spend working on your future.

By having a clear goal in mind, you will more likely finish feeling a sense of accomplishment and joy.

Chapter 2 Authenticity: Get to Know Who You Are at Your Core

Do you know who you are? Do you even have time to know who you are? Society talks about losing oneself, forgetting who we really are and that by forgetting who we are, our lives become inherently dull and less satisfying and fulfilling. Discovering your authentic self is key to knowing where to go next in your career and life.

> *"Authenticity is a collection of choices that we have to make every day. It's about the choice to show up and be real. The choice to be honest. The choice to let our true selves be seen."* – Brene Brown

Letting our authentic selves be seen is difficult if we forget who we are during the course of our lives and careers. I believe that forgetting who we are is part of a cycle of care or the path of a career. Care for ourselves is overridden at times by the need to care for others or the need to succeed in a career, but as with all cycles we can come back around to awareness and resume care for ourselves. Consider the cycle of parenthood or caring for a family member. Understand that we can go back and remember who we are.

> *"When we're growing up there are all sorts of people telling us what to do when really what we need is space to work out who to be."*
> – Elliot Page

This forgetting of self can also happen over the course of a career. It is extremely common for retirees to not know what to do with themselves after leading full and productive careers. The career cycle can come around to allow for discovery in retirement of who we are and what we wish to do. Some of my favorite clients over the years have been those starting their second or third careers or a new business after retirement.

Most importantly, getting to know who you are is not reserved for only those in transition, at the beginning, unexpected middle (layoff, job cuts), or end of a career. You can actively remember who you are at any point in the care or career cycles. So how do we go about remembering who we are when we are in the middle of our busy lives?

Frances Frei, Harvard Business School professor and co-author with Anne Morriss of the book *Unleashed: The Unapologetic Leader's Guide to Empowering Everyone Around You*, says that "Authenticity, logic, and empathy are the most vital skills an employee can have." If these are considered vital skills for an employee, then clearly being authentic is important during a career shift or transition.

Creating an authentic personal brand to help you get through the tasks needed for a successful job hunt takes dedication and time. The next big hurdle in figuring out who you are authentically is finding the time to be authentic.

The speed at which most of us run through life is becoming more and more rapid. The material wealth and possessions that marked success in the 1980s and 1990s have transitioned into success being measured by how booked our calendar is and how many responsibilities we manage. Busyness is now a competitive sport as reported through constantly pinging social media and over the top holiday cards as described by Brigid Schulte in *Overwhelmed: Work, Love and Play when No One has the Time*, a book filled with observations based on research about the time pressure of modern life. Her interview with Edson Rodriguez, a sociologist studying busy families in Los Angeles, sums up the societal pressures to maintain a busy life without time for ourselves. "We're validated by those around us living the same way and sanctioned if we aren't following this cultural expectation. The feeling is, if I'm not busy today, something's wrong."

As the Covid-19 pandemic shut down life as we know it, we were forced to reevaluate how we spend our time. Long commutes to work and school were no longer an option. Families that never ate meals together are now seeing each other at the dinner table almost every night. Long distance relationships with family and friends that were hard to maintain because we simply did not have the time were simplified and deepened through video conferencing. Budgets and meeting times were cut as teams realized meeting online worked as well as in person and cost much less in money and time.

This book was published while still in the middle of the pandemic; it remains to be seen whether the reacquainting with a slower pace of life will continue. Will the cultural shift towards less on the calendar continue or will the release after months (years) of some form of quarantine cause society to schedule even more? Will the benefit of fewer but more intense experiences create a better time value in the long run?

Regardless of the cultural shifts in time caused by the pandemic, the slowing down of our frenetic lives offers the opportunity to think about what we want out of our lives and careers. The concept of a well-planned sabbatical is not foreign or unusual and can be considered crucial for growth and innovation for high performing individuals and teams. Retreats, conventions, and sabbaticals offer structured time to explore who you are and what you want for the future.

Taking time away from your career and family to focus on who you are authentically at your core seems like a guilty luxury and unrealistic until you realize that your productivity is being chipped away by not staying true to yourself. In all aspects of your life, the truth of authenticity improves with reflection. Taking time to reflect on who you are leads to a better understanding of how to spend your precious and fleeting time.

Time is money as the saying goes. Time has become the most valuable of commodities as a local lottery billboard proclaims… "What would you do with all that time?" Money is not even mentioned in the advertisement. Tell me, what is more valuable than money? Time. Imagine if you could take the time to plan how you want to spend your time… as opposed to letting life and time pass you by. This is not an easy concept to grasp and an even harder practice to do. But for a moment imagine you had a choice.

Even a few minutes of mindfulness or meditation have shown improvements in productivity, mental capability, and self-awareness. Just imagine what spending dedicated time to discovering your authentic self could do for your career.

> *"It takes courage to grow up and become*
> *who you really are." – E.E. Cummings*

What to Do if You Get Stuck

It happens. People freeze. The fight or flight response fails. We are stuck, confused, and wondering what to do next. This applies to these exercises, but it also applies to everyday life. Writer's block and indecision happens to the best of us and the - oh so very human - rest of us. I personally have found these tools helpful when my mind is overwhelmed or I am so worried about something, I can't think straight, I can't get through a basic decision, or even fall asleep.

One person I worked with, "Ali," couldn't get past the first exercise. She literally was stuck. After a successful career in technology, she stepped out of corporate to raise her kids. Now that they were more self-sufficient, she was ready to step back into the workforce full-time. However, she lost herself in the busyness of life along the way. When she got the first exercise, she was stuck. This is a common occurrence for many people.

I thought long and hard about how to guide her through the exercise and came up with a few methods to become unstuck. These tools work like a reliable shovel to dig you out of the mud and push you up to dry ground to continue the journey. I included approximate times to help you decide which "getting unstuck" toolkit idea will work for you.

1. Think about the last time you felt calm, at peace, and relaxed. Close your eyes and imagine you are in that space and time. What does it sound or smell like? Mentally play over and over a 1-2-minute loop of the most relaxed moments. Take deep breaths and envision being there. Slowly tighten and release every muscle in your body starting with your toes and ending with your forehead, while laying or sitting still. Take 3 more deep breaths. Keep your eyes closed and imagine your relaxation space again. (Length of time is approximately 5-10 minutes).

2. When does time fly for you? What activity makes you lose track of time, creating a sense of flow? (Flow is a term coined by psychologist, Mihaly Csikzentmihalyi. In his book *Flow: The Psychology of Optimal Experience* he describes when one is completely focused on an activity so that they lose sense of time and are at the same time energized by the activity). Try to schedule an uninterrupted time to do this activity. Turn off your phone. Focus on the activity. If you must limit it to an hour, then do that but try to do it for at least an hour. (1-4 hours).

3. Do one uncomfortable thing. Walk instead of driving to the store. Call a friend of a friend that you would like to network with but have been waiting for the right moment. Eat a type of food you never have before. Listen to music you normally would not prefer. Read a book in a genre you don't typically buy or take out of the library. Try a different type of workout. Strike up a conversation with a stranger. By shaking up your normal routine, you will open different parts of your brain. (5-60 minutes).

4. Read a book. Not just any book. Read the book that you bought last year and meant to get to over the summer, but never did. Read the book your best friend or coworker loaned you and somehow forgot about in the shuffle of your home. Ask your roommate, spouse, kids, neighbor down the hall or other people you live with or near if they have a favorite book to lend you. This action actually works two-fold: it forces you to interact in a unique way with someone, it creates a situation where you will have to interact with them again to return the book and it gives you a discussion point to connect with them on it. Why are book clubs so popular? Besides the obvious food and beverage benefits, they allow us to connect with other humans. (5 minutes to 5 weeks).

5. Ask a close friend or sibling what they admire most about you. Simply hearing positive affirmations from someone you care about can change your entire outlook, giving you a safe and confident place to

continue to work. My family plays a game during long car trips when the agitation level reaches a high point. We call it "Warm Fuzzies." It is especially useful at defusing the tension between siblings or exhausted parents and small children. The first person says something kind about another person in the car. Then, that person says something kind about another person and so on until everyone has had at least 2 positive affirmations said to them. Warning: this may take practice and you will likely get push back from the kids, especially teens. Also, beware of backhanded compliments. Funny and witty, yes! Kind? Not so much. (15 minutes – 1 hour).

6. Practice mindfulness. Wonderful apps, podcasts and online YouTube videos can guide you through mindfulness exercises. Try one to experience life in the moment… to truly be present. "Mindfulness allows you to develop a broad set of cognitive and executive functions, raises self-awareness levels and facilitate emotional regulation, empowering individuals to substitute knee-jerk reactions with more conscious and ultimately more efficient behavior." Raffone, A., Srinivasan, N. *Mindfulness and Cognitive Functions Toward a Unifying Neurocognitive Framework*. (5 or more minutes).

After you have completed one of these activities, give yourself time to think about how you felt – maybe a day or more. Then, and only then, return to the exercise and try again. It may take a few attempts to find which method works best for you.

Self-Care + Self Awareness = Self Control

Knowing When to Leave or Say No

The work you are doing to learn more about yourself, your dreams, goals and more will take time. Finding time to do this important work may mean a few hard choices. But they are choices, which means it is within your ability to choose to spend time on creating your personal brand.

You have permission. My permission. Society's permission. Your streaming entertainment providers permission to… UNSUBSCRIBE. Walk away. Say NO!

Say no to what you don't need, don't want, never signed up for or can't believe you were forced to acknowledge.

Time is precious, so choose to step away from the parts of your life that:

- don't bring you joy,
- break from your mission in life,
- cause more harm than good, or
- take you further away from finding fulfillment.

Say no… say no often. Trust me it gets easier the more you say it. Like the eternally patient parent of a toddler in line at the grocery store. Say no. By saying no, you have more time to say yes to what you really want and need.

In *Drop the Ball*, Tiffany Dufu explains how she actively carved out a life she loves by systematically removing what she absolutely did not need to do herself.

In *Essentialism: The Disciplined Pursuit of Less* by Greg McKeown, a similar viewpoint is expressed by the author and ways to implement the concept across your life are given.

Again, we all lift and carry things, people, and responsibilities we don't need to. Many choices in life are more optional than they appear. More optional than required. So why do we let ourselves be controlled by a sense of what we *should* or *have to* do?

The first step in being authentic is knowing when to say no.

One of the hardest decisions to make is when to end a commitment. We are taught that quitting is wrong… a failure. But we are also taught that failure is a necessary part of the innovation process. Remember all the times you have failed and more importantly what those moments taught you about yourself and how you grew as person after having that failure.

We should not be afraid of failure. Instead we should look at failure as a required part of development. Failure is a necessary part of the innovation and growth mindset process.

Consider how NASA, National Aeronautics and Space Administration, chooses which candidates have the potential to be excellent astronauts. In the book *Mindset* by Carol S. Dweck, PH.D., Dr. Dweck talks about the NASA approach to using failure as a prerequisite for accepting applications. "When they were soliciting applications for astronauts, they rejected people with pure histories of success and instead selected people who had significant failures and bounced back from them." NASA specifically chose candidates that have failed in life since it provides an opportunity to see how they will handle and overcome challenges and problems in real life.

If we reconcile the act of quitting as more than a failure, we can better understand how to see it as a step in a long line of steps. By realizing it is more productive and useful to describe quitting as a leaving, moving on, or a growth opportunity. Quitting implies you have given up because you can no longer do the job or complete the tasks required of you. In many cases, moving on from a current responsibility will allow for the organization to grow as well. By leaving, you may open up an opportunity for a less experienced colleague to grow into the role you left. Aha! A chance to make the world a better place by allowing someone else to grow, learn, and stretch.

So, by leaving a role or job we are opening our ability to take on a role that may be even better suited for our unique personal brand.

Here are some questions to ask yourself before deciding to step away from a role:

- What is the original reason you started this role/activity? Is it still a valid reason?

- Who will benefit from you staying?

- Who will benefit from you leaving?

- What roles in your life will benefit once you no longer are committed to this role?

- What roles need more attention and time from you that you are unable to give because of this role?

Imagine you are at a party. The conversations are predictable. The food is good enough. The music is inconsequential. The people are interesting but not fascinating. Now imagine you get stuck in a corner forced to listen to an overly politically charged rant by a partygoer you barely know. A distasteful uncomfortable feeling comes over you as their views and arguments become more heated and one-sided by the minute. Does this scenario sound like the perfect time to excuse yourself to head to the bar, washroom or in response to a feigned gesture from a friend across the room? Does this moment sound like the perfect opportunity to leave? YES!

So why don't we leave when we know we should? Are we missing the obvious signs? What are the keys to knowing when you should step away?

The situation should reflect many of the statements listed below to qualify as the optimum time to go.

Signs you should leave:

- Coworkers are constantly criticizing your work without offering suggestions, time, resources, or efforts to help.

- You cannot honestly say you enjoy any aspect or part of the organization.

- You have naturally and/or with effort grown in skills in another direction from the role.

- The individual that brought you into the role or position is no longer with the organization.

- Any mentors or role models you have admired and modeled at the organization have left and no one has filled their place.

- When your emotional or motivational tank is empty, and you have run out of anything to give to others at the organization.

- You are not receiving recognition for the work you do.

Sometimes the hardest part of going is doing so despite the lack of any support from those around you to do just that. Reach outside the organization to find a supportive person, mentor, or friend to help you as you go through deciding if you should stay or go.

The common saying that when one door closes another door opens holds especially true with our time and commitments. By ending one role we are opening up our availability elsewhere.

Once you have decided to go, be sure to take time to refill your tank before moving on to another role. A sabbatical or vacation between roles is highly recommended to allow you to bring what makes you uniquely amazing to the new role.

Go Ahead and Brag About Yourself

One of the regular networking events I attend is organized with every person having two minutes to talk on a few specific topics about themselves and their work. The first few times I attended the event, I was so nervous that my elevator speech ended up sounding like a lot of bragging. I spoke way too quickly and had a hard time connecting with my listeners.

What frustrated me most about the situation was how I couldn't seem to focus on the message that would actually explain what makes me unique in my field. I was given a real opportunity to shine and do a little appropriate bragging and I just couldn't find the balance between bragging enough and too much bragging.

Bragging can be uncomfortable for everyone involved. In the wrong situation or context, bragging can seem inappropriate, garish, and immature. We all know people that upon meeting for the first time come across as self-centered and unaware of how their bragging makes others feel. Saying something positive about yourself and others is part of meeting and networking. However, not inquiring about the person on the other end of the conversation can make you seem shallow.

So why is it okay to brag about yourself? Because we need to brag or risk missing the opportunity to share what we can do to help others. Bragging within limits is also necessary to your success, happiness, and growth as an individual. No one ever gets a positive response after a job interview without saying at least a few positive things about themselves.

So, *when* is it okay to brag about yourself?

The best times to brag about yourself are when you are explicitly asked to brag about yourself. An organization requests a bio for materials used to market you as a panelist for an upcoming webinar. Brag away! You are asked during an interview for a job or on a show what makes you special or why they should hire you. Brag away! You are at an organized networking event and they ask you to showcase what makes you great. By all means, brag away!

These opportunities are designed to help you share who you are authentically and help the other person or audience make decisions about whether to hire you or consider you an expert worth listening to.

Regarding my personal networking example above, I gradually got better at the balance of appropriate bragging by watching and listening to what other members of the group said and how they reacted, but I still consider this a skill to continuously work on as part of a growth mindset.

Practice made the situation much more comfortable. I picked up on a few key bragging guidelines during this time from many of the more eloquent speakers. The situation most crucial to appropriate bragging is the job interview.

During a job interview, a lot can be gained or lost based on how you react, what you say, and how the interviewer interprets what you say.

Exactly, *how* can you brag in a way that helps instead of hurting you or others around you?

A few guidelines for bragging during an interview:

1. Speak the truth.

Lying your way through an interview is never worth doing and only causes confusion or negative results. Chances are – if they as the interviewer have prepared well – they have already looked up the information from multiple sources including the Internet and are simply confirming with you for a well-timed (and easily repeatable to the hiring committee) sound bite.

2. Stay focused.

Brag about what your interviewer and audience are most interested in hearing from you. You may be the world's best parallel parker, but a job interview for an accounting position will most likely want to focus on your history of successful projects in finance, budgeting, or other related business fields.

3. Highlight with Facts.

Sharing specific numbers or facts as well as offering a reference or link to a reputable website featuring the evidence of your excellence goes a long way in establishing your credibility. If you decreased the time it takes to bring a new product to market by 35%, increased sales by 125% over a year, increased engagement by 15% over last quarter on your brand's social media, saved the company $250,000 over 3 months, brag away! Be specific and choose examples that are relevant to the skills needed for the position. Don't worry if you are switching industries. Saving time, money, and resources are always appreciated. And growth in sales or output is necessary to justify a new hire. Make their job easy.

As uncomfortable as bragging can feel, it is part of the process of promoting your personal brand authentically and successfully to get the type of work or opportunity that brings you fulfillment.

Practice bragging with a trusted colleague, roommate, family member or friend. Explain that you are in the process of getting to know yourself better and want to be prepared for the next time someone asks what you do during a networking event or in a work situation.

Then, ask them what they would like to brag about. You may just learn something amazing about them that you never would have known otherwise.

Remembering and Celebrating Your Talents

A talent is something for which you have a natural affinity. Do not worry if you are not the best in the world at this talent. Choose talents that others have recognized your ability and for which you may have received awards or accolades.

One client, "Jennie," fondly remembers spending summers at her grandmother's home in upstate New York helping in the garden. They would clip and arrange fresh flowers every week to brighten the kitchen and even bring flowers to neighbors. Today, Jennie is a graphic designer and it wasn't until she started working on her personal brand that she realized the skills she used as a child directly impacted her career. Understanding her natural talents and where they first exhibited themselves helps Jennie as she considers how to approach a project or task.

If you are having a hard time finding your talent or think your talent is in some way a negative, don't worry about it. What you consider negative could very well be an asset for a hiring professional who needs that talent in an employee.

For a volunteer organization in my neighborhood, I accepted a position on the board a few years ago to help with marketing. The person who had the position before me was exceptionally good at detail work, but not so good at teamwork, customer service, or big picture thinking. Being detail oriented is not a top talent of mine. At first, I was put out by the number of times I was corrected by my predecessor for the first few months, thinking it was because she was micromanaging or simply did not train me well. Then I realized that she was the perfect predecessor to follow in that she had already improved what the role could do for the organization in her way and now I could move the role forward even further without having to reinvent the wheel. I would normally have considered her detail-oriented nature as a limitation or roadblock; however, her talent is what helped me navigate the tasks I needed to complete until I knew enough to create my own way.

Consider looking at unique parts of you that may at first seem negative, but when considered as talents that you are exceptionally good at, will make more sense in painting a complete picture of who you are and what you bring to your work.

Listing your talents can seem like bragging. However, if you consider talents to be useful assets that help you find purpose and enjoyment in life through success, you will more easily be able to highlight and share your unique talents during a career shift.

The Importance of Pride

Pride is defined by Dictionary.com as "pleasure or satisfaction taken in something done by or belonging to oneself or believed to reflect credit upon oneself."

Being proud of who you are and what you have accomplished plays two main roles in personal branding. First, it acknowledges the effort and expertise behind your accomplishments and achievements. Second, it acts as a self-fulfilling motivator to encourage you to continue to act in the way that allows you to succeed. It feels good to accomplish a task that you set out to do. It feels even better when the accomplishment creates a sense of pride in yourself and your work.

Chapter 2 Exercises

The set of exercises below will help you learn what *talents*, *skills*, and *personality traits* define you. These exercises simplify the task by giving you a roadmap to find your true authentic self.   This journey is unique for every person. If an exercise does not resonate with you, read my "What to Do-if-You-are-Stuck" section over from earlier in this chapter and if you are still having trouble… skip it. It is okay to move on. However, the more exercises you complete, the closer you will get to understanding your unique, authentic personal brand.

Note: These answers will be used later in the book, so don't hold back on writing down as many answers as you can. Including a lot of answers will let you have many to choose from when you reach the later exercises.

Talents

Look back on yourself as a child, teen, and college student. What did you love to do in your free time during weekends, summers, holidays, camps, and afterschool? What hobbies, sports, household activities like cooking or organizing, crafts, arts – performing and/or media, collections, games, or other activities did you love to do?

List as many as you can and draw pictures or diagrams if it helps.

"Success means we go to sleep at night knowing that our talents and abilities were used in a way that served others." –
Marianne Williamson

Now considering the activities that you consider to be one of your talents, list 5 things even now that you know you are genuinely good at and bring you joy:

1.

2.

3.

4.

5.

Note any similarities in the activities listed above. What do they have in common with each other? Which one stands out from the rest? Circle the one that brings you the most joy.

According to Workable, one of the world's top hiring platforms, talents are "a natural aptitude, an inner quality that emerges effortlessly" so choosing your top talents may require asking co-workers or friends to notice them. The effortless nature of a talent makes it seem to not be as amazing or worthy of attention, but that is exactly why you need to write down a list of your talents when starting your career search.

Remembering Moments of Pride

Think of a time you felt great pride: business, scholastic, sports, work, art, performance, or accomplishment. Having these carefully chosen and stored memories of a time of pride helps us when we doubt ourselves.

Consider creating a list of one or two words near your workspace that describe moments of pride in your life or even using a photo, trophy, or other memento to remind you of your moment of pride. It is not uncommon to see framed medals from races or jerseys or community award certificates or even diplomas in an office. These are symbols of the hard work required to earn them and the pride we felt upon achieving each.

When you start a new project or question your abilities, remember those times to give yourself confidence and strength. Even filling out these exercises can create a sense of pride as you list the qualities that make you uniquely wonderful.

"Don't wait until you reach your goal to be proud of yourself. Be proud of every step you take."
– Karen Salmansohn

Complete the following phrases to help you find your talents.

I have been told I am incredibly talented at…

My greatest talent is…

The one talent I am known for is…

Think of at least 3 times when your showed true talent. Now focus on the strongest memory. What talent did you show to earn that sense of pride? Feel free to draw a picture, chart, or diagram to explain. If you have a photo or trophy representing that time of pride, use a printout to help you remember.

Skills

Skill, as defined by Webster's Dictionary, is "the ability to use one's knowledge effectively and readily in execution or performance." My translation is that skills are a list of abilities that you do well and that have been improved through use and study. Unlike talents, skills require practice, study, and education to become proficient.

The purpose of this exercise is to see what you bring to the table. What are the unique skills that allow you to do your job, succeed at a task and make you a valuable contributor to a group, corporation, team, or organization?

> *"We must have perseverance and, above all, confidence in ourselves. We must believe we are gifted for something and that this thing must be attained." – Marie Curie*

The important difference between talents and skills is that skills require persistence of practice and study, whereas talents are innate and naturally show themselves without necessarily needing practice or study. You should be proud of the commitments you have made to learn and develop a skill.

Below is a list of skills. Circle the ones that are most true for you.

Use the following sentence starters to help.

I am very skillful at ….

I am known for being good at…

People know they can rely on my….

List of Skills

Listening

Adapting or being flexible

Coaching or directing

Reading

Conflict resolution

Maintaining focus

Creativity

Project management

Following a recipe

Perseverance

Decision Making

Delegating

Doing laundry

Hospitality

Communicating

Motivating

Managing teams

Mentoring others

Shopping

Problem solving or troubleshooting

Strategic Thinking

Cooking/baking

Stress management

Parenting

Organizing

Time management

Research

Financial management

Performing repetitive tasks

Critical questioning

Following directions on a road

Writing

DIY home projects

Teamwork

Developing & maintaining relationships

Taking initiative or action

Presenting to a group

Cleaning a home

Driving

Event planning

First aid

Budgeting

Home decorating

Computer or social media

Sports

Making people laugh

Studying

Travelling

Caring for people or pets

Fundraising

"You are allowed to be both a masterpiece & a work in progress simultaneously." – Sophia Bush

I love this quote. It reminds me that we are always developing ourselves. And more importantly that we should not be too hard on ourselves and practice self-compassion.

Discovering your personal brand is intimate, emotional work. It requires a lot of thinking and dedicated time. This is not light work and turning the camera lens towards yourself is not the lighthearted selfie on Instagram, but a long deep documentary with all the flaws bared and all the details exposed to the light.

Practicing the compassion and understanding of yourself will allow you to be more compassionate and understanding towards others.

A business or relationship thrives if based on mutual respect, understanding and compassion. Consider using mindfulness or meditation practices that focus on compassion if you are having a hard time giving yourself a break.

Highlight Your Skills

Imagine participating in a team building exercise at work or on a reality TV show. What skills would you offer to make the team succeed? If it helps, think about yourself five to ten years ago. What skills have stayed the same? What have you added?

List 3 skills that you are good at and came naturally to you. These can come from the list above.

1.

2.

3.

List 3 skills that you worked hard to learn through education or persistent practice and are still confident in your ability to do them. Natural ability is wonderful, but some skill sets require learning and practice to master.

Just because you had to work hard to be great at a skill, does not mean it is not a strong part of who you are.

1.

2.

3.

Personality traits

For this section, it is important to focus on traits you personally consider as positive. Ignore any negative thoughts or personality traits that you are not proud of. Part of understanding your authentic self is being aware of what personality traits will help you succeed and become your best self. Negative or self-deprecating traits and thoughts need to be put aside for the moment to create your personal brand.

Beware of the internal naysayer; that ugly voice inside your head that says you are not good enough. You are enough! You are good enough!

Negativity can bring anxiety and fear. While a fear of failure is an excellent motivator towards getting work done, anxiety, negative stress, and negativity are counter-productive to achieving results.

I am not in any way suggesting to completely ignore the less than wonderful traits you or I possess. I am simply suggesting that you become aware of who you really are.

Just don't dwell on the negativity for longer than you need to.

Self-awareness can be achieved with self-compassion and without self-destruction.

"I think self-awareness is probably the most important thing toward being a champion." – Billie Jean King

Below is a list of personality traits. Circle the ones that are most true for you.

Use the following sentence starters to help:

I can best be described as …

The words I think of when I look in the mirror are ….

Managers, team members or leaders have described me as….

List of Personality Traits

Active or energetic	Ambitious
Admirable	Articulate
Adventuresome	Athletic
Agreeable	Attractive

Authentic	Educated
Balanced	Elegant
Benevolent	Eloquent
Calm	Empathetic
Caring	Enthusiastic
Cerebral	Extrovert
Challenging	Fair
Charismatic	Faithful
Cheerful	Firm
Clever	Flexible
Colorful	Forgiving
Compassionate	Friendly
Competitive	Frugal
Confident	Fun-loving
Conscientious	Gentle
Considerate	Genuine
Contemplative	Glamorous
Cooperative	Good-natured
Courageous	Gracious
Courteous	Grateful
Creative	Hardworking
Decisive	Healthy
Discreet	Idealistic
Dramatic	Imaginative
Dutiful	Independent

Innovative	Perfectionist
Intelligent	Persuasive
Introvert	Playful
Intuitive	Polished
Kind	Popular
Liberal	Practical
Logical	Principled
Loving	Private
Loyal lovable	Protective
Methodical	Prudent
Meticulous	Punctual
Moderate	Rational
Modern	Realistic
Modest	Reflective
Neat	Religious
Obedient	Resourceful
Objective observation	Respectful
Old-fashioned	Responsible
Open	Sage
Optimistic	Scholarly
Organized	Selfless
Passionate	Self-sufficient
Patient	Serious
Peaceful	Sexy
Perceptive	Shrewd

Simple   Thorough

Social   Tidy

Sophisticated   Tolerant

Stylish   Understanding

Subtle   Urbane

Sweet   Vivacious

Sympathetic   Warm

Tasteful

Personality Traits of Your Closest Confidants

"It's the friends that you can call up at 4 a.m. that matter." – Marlene Dietrich

What a wonderfully truthful statement! What would you do without the people in your life that you can rely on... especially when a crisis strikes in the middle of the night?

Make a point in the next week to personally thank each of those people in your everyday life that you know you can rely on. A few words of gratitude go a long way. I try to never take for granted the people in my life that I have been able to rely on. What I find amusing is when those dear friends ask for a favor and seem surprised that I will happily do whatever it takes to help... how could I not, after all they have done for me.

List your four closest friends or trusted colleagues.

In parentheses after each name, put three personality traits that describe that person.

Describe what you admire about their personalities. Focus only on the traits that are positive and hopefully you have seen help them succeed in their own lives.

Friends (personalities)

1.

2.

3.

4.

Looking over this list, are there any personality traits that you share with them? Which personality traits do you share with one or more of them?

List the personality traits you share.

Create Your Core List

Next, gather the information in the previous exercises into one place using the Core List template below. Listing what you learned about yourself in the exercises above will help clarify who you are at your very core. Essentially, you will create a core list that describes your authentic self.

Try to finish this next exercise before taking a long break. Avoid overthinking your answers to the exercises you have already completed. It is more important to find the answers that come easily and obviously. However, if you feel this is a difficult part to complete. Go ahead and start reading the next chapter. If you skip this exercise now, be sure to come back to the first set of exercises before starting Part Two (Chapters 4-6) as each section builds on the prior section.

To understand your personal brand and who you are at your core... to find your authentic self, you will need to simplify your results from all these exercises into an easy to read template. The below template offers a consolidation of the self-awareness you have worked towards in these chapters.

Looking back on your answers to the earlier exercises, fill in the lists below. If you need to add a fourth to a list or only want to list two, that will work as well. Be honest with yourself about which are the most important traits for explaining who you are… not who you think you should be or who you think others want you to be. Simply be clear about who you are at your core.

Your Core List Template

My Top 3 Talents

1.

2.

3.

My Top 3 Skills

1.

2.

3.

My Top 3 Personality Traits

1.

2.

3.

Describe Who You Are

Using the top talents, skills and personality traits that define you, create a one to three sentence description of who you are.

Don't overthink it.

Pretend you are telling a close friend what you learned about yourself in the process. Speak in straight forward, easy to understand words. Don't worry about stating what seems obvious if it is authentically you.

> *"You are the one that possesses the keys to your being. You carry the passport to your own happiness."*
> – Diane von Furstenberg

If it helps, use the sentence starters at the beginning of the talents, skills, and personality traits exercises to create the description. The point of this exercise is to start giving you the words to share your personal brand with others. Sharing who you are at your core, your why, your true self. This is only the beginning of sharing your story and your brand.

Here are some additional sentence starters to help you begin:

"I have been told I am very talented at…"

"My greatest talent is…"

"The one talent I am known for is…"

"I am very skillful at …."

"I am known for being really good at…"

"People know they can rely on my…."

"I can best be described as …"

"The words I think of when I look in the mirror are …."

"Managers, team members or leaders have described me as…."

Chapter 3 Find Your Inspiration: Look Back to Move Forward

This chapter is focused on helping you discover your favorite work and life activities.

Only by understanding what you enjoy and look forward to can you decide what to schedule or work towards for your life and career. It is also intended to give you hope that you can spend your time doing what you love.

How you spend your time can be divided into three activity categories: Work, Commitments, and Hobbies.

> *"Find out what you like doing best and*
> *get someone to pay you for it."*
> *– Katharine Whitehorn*

Work

Work is often how we define or identify ourselves. Consider when you meet someone at a party. After their name and perhaps how they know the host, what is usually the next piece of information you share? What you do for a living.

Work is also how we and others define or describe ourselves as compared to others. The prestige of our title, department or company can alter our internal view and value of ourselves, as well as the view and value perceived by those around us.

Just considering the choices of title to put on a business card can have huge ramifications. A perusal of your LinkedIn connections and their current titles makes for interesting research. What is Chief Happiness Officer anyway?

A quick side note: Chief Happiness Officer is another term used for the official title of Chade-Meng Tan, the Jolly Good Fellow of Google. His book *Search Inside Yourself: The Unexpected Path to Achieving Success, Happiness (and World Peace)* has revolutionized how corporations and people look at applying mindfulness to their lives and work structures. I think we should all aspire to someday have a title that can change the world. What will yours be?

A job title can define the job, status, or responsibilities. A title can indicate who makes decisions and who reports to whom. It helps everyone understanding the dynamics of a company and implies who holds the final decision-making power. The ultimate stakeholder can be masked by a title without the implied power.

Work also says a lot about who we are and gives a glimpse into our personal brand. Depending on the work type, you can learn a lot about a person's skills, education, and lifestyle. The type of work can clearly indicate whether the person works mostly with their hands or their minds. It can also tell what that individual is likely to be wearing to work and the environment where they work. The type of work can also suggest the days, times and seasons associated with their lives.

As a result of many parts of our lives being determined by our jobs, we cannot help but be defined by what we do for work. So if work so deeply defines who we are and many of the decisions we make about our lives, then shouldn't we spend a lot more time and energy choosing what best fits with who we are and our needs, wants, desires and dreams?

Shouldn't we aim for a career that fulfills us in every way? A career that gives us satisfaction while doing it. A job that uses the skills we worked hard and sacrificed much to acquire. A position that inspires us to be the best version of ourselves and to continuously keep learning and growing. This is the good stuff that gets us out of bed each morning and eventually makes the world a better place.

The first logical step for moving your personal brand forward is to look back at all the work you have done in the past. Examine what you did at each job and, more importantly, what you enjoyed or did not enjoy about each position. Looking at your past work will let you collect clues as to what you could be doing in the future. Valuable clues indicate where you will find success in work, fulfillment and finally help you examine every aspect of a career from commute to labor to co-workers and colleagues. The clues when viewed together give a rich and full picture of what work should be for each of us.

Commitments

Ahh, commitments. Commitments are parts of our lives that at times can bring us great joy and happiness and also stress, and yet are a part of our lives that we can't quit or leave for a newer, better opportunity. These parts of our lives are items and obligations we can't ignore or put off.

Commitments are the parts of our life we don't have a choice or the option to change right now or sometimes ever.

Yes, many of these commitments are the best parts of life and the reason for living. However, realistically some commitments can at times make us feel trapped, stuck, or exist as a continuous stream of mundane tasks. Some commitments can be positive and some negative and, for quite a few, they can oscillate between positive and negative. Either way, uplifting or consuming, commitments are there whether we like them or not.

There are three important points to consider about commitments.

First, you can't change it... at least not now. (I will get back to the ability to change in point three.)

Second, given that you can't change it, you might as well make the best of the situation and choose to accept it. Look for the bright spots or focus on the parts that inspire and motivate you or bring you joy. And let go of the negative feelings of pain, guilt, or dislike that realistically you cannot do anything about right now. Give up resentment and anger. Let go of frustration, helplessness, and hopelessness. If you can't do anything about it, then why let your feelings hold you back? I need to share a confession. Letting go is hard to do for me personally. I know that if I don't choose to let go of my frustration and bad feelings, I will never be the best version of myself. And I must accept that and give myself a break. And you should too. You will have to keep trying even if you don't get it right every time. It's okay.

Third, remember that many commitments are not permanent and in time will change. This third point gives you the opportunity to step back, take a deep breath, and gain perspective even when you feel completely overwhelmed. Be kind to yourself and, in turn, you can be kind to others.

Years later you may look back on your commitments that at the time seemed to never end as the role that gave you the strength to get you through all that came after.

> *"What doesn't kill you makes you stronger." – Kelly Clarkson.*

The original quote is attributed to the German Philosopher, Friedrich Nietzsche.

> *"That which does not kill us, makes us stronger." – Nietzsche*

But Kelly Clarkson sang it so much better. Anyway, if it doesn't make you stronger, you will at least be more empathetic when you see others struggle.

When I start working with clients, we discuss the realities of having a job that pays the bills. We all need a source of income to provide a roof over our heads, food on the table, clothes on our backs, enough access to medical care and whatever else your life necessities are. It is very realistic and okay to have a job that you don't completely love because it takes care of some or all those necessities. That is a commitment.

Some examples of commitments are being a primary caregiver for someone or something. Another example is if you have a medical condition that requires time to manage and be responsible for. Another example is a role in which you are serving a community for a specific length of time or term. There are more examples that I am certain will come to mind as you examine your life and look at others' lives as to what a commitment can be.

The important part of this section is to understand the level of responsibility and lack of ability to change (for now) that signifies your obligation to that commitment.

Hobbies

Why is it important to look at your hobbies? Well, part of creating a truly authentic personal brand is looking at all aspects of how you spend your time and where you might be seen in the world: online or in real life. Hobbies are often the resume endnote or cocktail topic that most ingratiate us to people. Hobbies make us seem at once more interesting and more human... more relatable.

Hobbies are things you do for fun in your leisure time (even if no one else would find it fun). A friend once shared a story that she was at a formal dinner of women in her industry and as an ice breaker they went around the table listing their hobbies. When it came to her turn, she said reading. Now this friend is a highly intelligent person, whose idea of pleasure reading is hard hitting articles on high level thinking about society and work. I always admire her choice to read intellectual, substantive material. She was scoffed at by the Alpha female at the table, who made fun of her for not having a hobby. Success is so competitive that we now need to prove our hobbies are worth doing! What!?

After hearing the uncomfortable dinner party hobby story, I thought about the hobby of the Alpha female – golfing – like any working parent has five hours of time on a weekend to ignore their kids and spouse and trudge around a perfectly manicured fairway. And I love golfing, but we all need to prioritize our time. While considering the Alpha female's comments, I theorized that she had missed the point completely.

Hobbies are intrinsically for our own enjoyment. We don't normally get paid to do them. We certainly don't feel obligated to do them to prove something to someone else. Who cares what you choose for your hobby? Relax and be grateful we live in an age of so many choices to spend our free or leisure time.

Gaetano DiNardi, in an HBR.org post, *Why You Should Work Less and Spend More Time on Hobbies*, explains the financial implications of a lack of hobbies: "When people don't have time for hobbies, businesses pay a price. Hobbies can make workers substantially better at their jobs."

In very real terms, being able to enjoy and take time for a hobby allows us the ability to do our jobs better. Doing our jobs better translates into higher levels of performance and results in more profit.

"When you recover or discover something that nourishes your soul and brings joy, care enough about yourself to make room for it in your life." – Jean Shinoda Bolen

If you are having trouble with this section's exercises because you don't feel that you have a hobby, think more broadly.

A hobby can be as simple as imagining what you would do if you had all the money in the world, or an unlimited amount of time and energy. A hobby can be choosing at least one museum to visit every time you travel to a new city for work or pleasure. A hobby could be trying to find the best pizza within 100 miles of your home. Photography is considered a hobby and chances are you carry around with you a smart phone with at least 3 cameras and multiple ways to post your captured images. Social media is even considered a hobby. Cooking, dancing, listening to a genre of music, playing video games… all of these can be hobbies.

Research by Girija Kaimail, EdD, assistant professor, and Kendra Ray, a doctoral student, both in Drexel's College of Nursing and Health Professions, showed "that just about 45 minutes of free art-making in a studio attended by an art therapist was enough to increase a person's self-efficacy – a term used to describe a person's confidence in themselves and their ability to complete tasks."

Any activity that consumes your time and attention is important to consider for the following exercises. Which category – work, commitment, or hobby – will determine the flexibility of that time and attention. The category will clearly indicate where a substantial change can and should take place in your life. Maybe not right now, but eventually.

Learning to Let Go

Ah, Elsa, how many true moments of wisdom have we gained from that one song, "Let it go!" from the movie *Frozen*. As a mom, I have watched and listened to this song hundreds of times (it was the first song my deaf daughter heard the day she got her hearing aids). And each time the message changes slightly depending on what is going on around me that day. Experiencing the freedom and release expressed in that song combined with the ability to be authentic certainly sounds like someone embracing their personal brand.

The words of the song are particularly resonating with me now… as I write this in the middle of months of shelter at home during the pandemic. Managing and watching the emotions, reactions, and negotiations of my roommates (a.k.a., kids/husband) is an enlightening lesson in who can and who can't let it go. The ability to let go is not a given for everyone. Some people work through uncertainty by pushing everyone around them harder than others, making you want to scream at them to drop it already. So why is it so hard to simply let it go?

"The key is to let go of two things: grasping and aversion. Grasping is when the mind desperately holds on to something and refuses to let it go. Aversion is when the mind desperately keeps something away and refuses to let it come. These two qualities are flip sides of each other. Grasping and aversion together account for a huge percentage of the suffering we experience, perhaps 90 percent, maybe even 100 percent." Chade-Meng Tan, Search Inside Yourself: The Unexpected Path to Achieving Success, Happiness.

To simplify, let go of what is holding you back, especially things that are out of your control. Seriously, sometimes you need to realize when to stop stressing over the static, stubborn parts of life. Change what you can. Let go of the rest!

Embrace the release of venting! Yes, venting! A recommendation… focus on venting in the comfort of a journal to avoid the confusion, frustration or misguided anger at your roommates or coworkers if done out of context. Then, if appropriate, consider sharing with a therapist or confidante.

The act of letting it go can be quite difficult, especially when you have the best of intentions behind *not* letting it go. It is far easier to hold onto a grudge or resentment because you just can't understand why releasing control over a person, idea, event, or project may improve the situation.

"Almost everything will work again if
you unplug it for a few minutes,
including you." – Anne Lamott

Conversely if you are the person being controlled by another's inability to let go, you may find yourself doubting yourself, your decisions, and your abilities... leading to despair. Do not despair.

There is hope even when dealing with a teammate, manager, or coworker who refuses to let it go. One of the most important takeaways from this book should be to practice self-compassion. Self-compassion is a form of letting go... letting go of the harsh judgement we place on ourselves when it should really be let go. It is okay to give yourself a break.

One summer, I had the pleasure of cohosting Intentional Focus Retreats with O mag insider, founder of the *52 Phenomenal Women Project*, host of the *Speaking of Phenomenal* Podcast and professional photographer, Amy Boyle. One of our many wonderful, wise, and gifted guest speakers, Dr. Kate Roberts, spoke about knowing when enough is enough. My paraphrase of her guidance after the time we spent together at the retreat can be summed up in the following affirmation:

My best is good enough.

Just think about that for a moment. What if you lived your life trying your best and then realized at the end of each day that you are enough, your actions are enough, and what you give to others is enough? Consider how empowering that would be towards gaining more time in your life.

*"And now that you don't have to be
perfect, you can be good."
– John Steinbeck*

Stop getting in the way of your own progress. We can get in the way of ourselves by striving for perfection without a purpose, only seeing one solution, or preventing the innovation that occurs with random trial-and-error.

So how can you actively learn to let go?

Keep a worry journal. At night before falling asleep, write down all the things you are concerned about or worried about. Be mindful of which ones are out of your control or can wait until a later day to focus on. Let the process of writing remove the worry from your mind, so you can rest.

Repeat the words to yourself over and over: My best is good enough.

Delegate. Look back at your calendar from the last week. List all of the tasks you expected yourself to accomplish. Try to find tasks that do not need to be done now or ever. Determine which tasks can and should be done by someone else. Let the ones that are not essential go!

Mentally imagine whatever you are refusing to let go as a helium balloon. Release the string of that balloon and watch it float away until you no longer see it. What is remarkable about this visualization is that, like most things in life, when you gain some perspective by moving away from an event or situation, you often see how small and insignificant it is in the vast scheme of things.

Look for inspiration in music, movies, and books for characters that exist without time constraints. The quote below from *The Curious Case of Benjamin Button* (a movie about a man who ages backwards from old age to infancy) emphasizes how time cannot stop our choice to change ourselves and our lives.

"For what it's worth: it's never too late or, in my case, too early to be whoever you want to be. There's no time limit, stop whenever you want. You can change or stay the same, there are no rules to this thing. We can make the best or the worst of it. I hope you make the best of it. And I hope you see things that startle you. I hope you feel things you never felt before. I hope you meet people with a different point of view. I hope you live a life you're proud of. If you find that you're not, I hope you have the courage to start all over again." — Eric Roth, The Curious Case of Benjamin Button Screenplay.

Create a goodbye ritual of writing down something you need to let go and ripping it to shreds. Or tossing it into a campfire.

An important part of finding what brings you fulfillment is to learn to let go of what does not.

Chapter 3 Exercises

Inspiration provides the needed boost to accomplish great things! The situations that inspire you and the activities you are most drawn to show where your passions lie. Being passionate about something gives you the energy, focus, and perseverance to be exceptional when doing the work or activity. This ability to generate excellence in execution leads to success and fulfillment from doing your best.

The exercises for Chapter 3 let you know which activities:

- stir your soul,

- inspire you to do and be more, and

- bring you great joy, satisfaction, and fulfillment.

The activities that light a fire within you are the activities to focus the most on as you continue through the exercises in this chapter and throughout the book.

By understanding what work, volunteering, activities, and hobbies bring you joy, purpose, and inspiration, you will be able to seek out future opportunities that give you true fulfillment.

"I've learned that making a living is not the same thing as making a life."
– Maya Angelou

Work & Volunteering Roles

List, with a brief description of your role, the last three to seven work positions or volunteer positions you have had and what you liked best and least about each. If it is easier, choose the positions that have had the biggest impact in your life. Some people are more in touch with what has recently happened, whereas others are more in tune with the parts of their lives that have had the biggest emotional, financial, or experiential impact. Choose the roles that most resonate with you.

Use the following template for each role or position for work or volunteering.

Role Template

Organization name:

     Your role:

     Your favorite part:

     Your least favorite part:

     What skills or knowledge you gained from the role:

     Who you helped:

     What achievements or results were accomplished through your actions (projects, goals, awards):

Hobbies

Hobbies exist purely for our pleasure and enjoyment. The smallest activity can be a hobby. Hobbies have been known to grow into businesses and careers, especially as the concept of always having a side hustle and multiple income sources become more prevalent.

List your Hobbies.

What do you love about each hobby?

How did you discover or who helped you start doing this hobby? Tell a story about the first time you tried this hobby or what events occurred that led you to make this an important part of your time. As an added bonus, reach out to the person that inspired you to start the hobby and thank them for bringing you joy.

When you are preparing to do this hobby, what inspires or excites you the most?

What do you look forward to doing?

What makes you happy just planning to do it?

What is your favorite part about the hobby?

Commitments

Beyond our jobs and hobbies, a variety of activities take up our time and fill our days. Some of these we choose. Some we feel we have no choice but to do them out of obligation. In this exercise, focus on what takes up your time that did not fall into the categories listed above. By accounting for your hours, you will gain a better understanding of how these activities shape your personal brand.

Think about how you spend your weeknights, weekends, and vacations.

What activities do you spend the most time doing?

What activities do you plan the rest of your day around?

Imagine you are looking at a calendar for your year, what are the items that come up most frequently?

What are the calendar events that make you smile/dread when you see them on next week's agenda?

"If you obey all the rules, you miss all the fun." – Katharine Hepburn

Time Mapping (Mind Mapping Your Time)

In this exercise, you will use a mind map to visualize how you spend your time each year. I use this exercise every January to plan out how I want to spend my time in the coming year.

By looking at the activities, jobs, roles, responsibilities, hobbies, etc. that make up your life on one page, you can easily see which ones need more time, which ones to eliminate, and where you need to add more.

Some categories to consider adding: your career, volunteering, each of the family members/others you are a caregiver for, pets, hobbies, activities, clubs, organizations you belong to, career planning (networking events), self-care (workouts, therapy, medical appointments), home care (bill paying, housework, home repair or scheduling).

After creating the major categories, create branches off each to further explain all the time usage needed for each part of your life. Finally, look at all the different parts of your life or career and consider what your life would be like without each part. Prioritize your favorites (and the one that pays the bills of course). Which ones make you happy? Which cause stress and anxiety? Which ones have changed? Have you changed so that certain categories no longer make sense to keep in your life?

Some years I realize that my clients are the bulk of my time, other years my volunteer work, and still other years my family. What is absolutely amazing is when looked at as a whole, it is easy to pick out the activities that you would be completely fine getting rid of. Most of the time you can't just drop a role or responsibility instantly, but you can start to make plans to remove it from your life.

I am also surprised when basic needs like self-care or time with friends gets left off or minimized. Remember that you need to put on your own oxygen mask and fill your tank first. Then and only then can you help others and have the energy to bring your best to all areas of your life.

After this exercise, you may need to add or revise your answers to the previous exercises about work, hobbies, and commitments. That is completely to be expected and part of the process. These are all working documents that change as you pick up new roles or remove old ones.

The following is an example of a time map.

Time Map

A Time map is a Mind Map that organizes your life on one page. Start by creating circles of the different parts of your life: work, family, hobbies, volunteering, etc. Next, create branches with the responsibilities that require your time for each one. Create this time map once a year to keep track of how you are using your time and learn where you want to change how to use your time in the future.

Your Life

family
- spouse
- kids
- home & bills
- parents & pets

friends
- softball league
- book club
- annual friends weekend

self-care
- nutrition
- meditation
- exercise
- health

work
- new project
- annual report
- career
- project 1

volunteer work
- committee work
- gala
- monthly meeting

copyright by Heather H. Bennett

85

Part Two: Researching, Finding and Preparing for Your Next Role

What if for most of the year you could do what you love?

While reimagining what my own work-life could look like, I had to learn to focus on the projects that worked best for my clients and for me. Helping clients find meaningful work that utilized their unique skills and experience is both fun and fulfilling. I love what I do. But I had to figure out where that work would come from and where there was a need for my skills. Finding out that people needed someone to help them understand their personal brand so they would be able to find and do work they loved took years and was lifechanging. It gave me work I love!

Often choosing a job that you love seems overwhelming because we are trained to follow logical career paths that stem from our education and past work experience. Separating your skills and talents from what is the logical next job in your career helps you to find new opportunities outside of what is typical. Try focusing on your skills and what other roles would use those skills.

Simply understanding what jobs await someone with your qualifications requires a little research. And then, after finding out what you want to do, figuring out what you need to do to get you there. Research where you could go and then prepare for success once you get there.

A few years ago, I had the opportunity to work with a college student just finishing his search for the ideal summer job after his freshman year. "Roger" had been pursuing a degree in business at a large state university and wanted to find a summer job that would continue to develop his business acumen. He kept returning to the idea of what he thought he would do after he graduated three years later. As we looked at each opportunity individually, I helped him understand that focusing on that far in the future would be a roadblock that limited his options long term and for the summer. He had narrowed his options down to three summer positions.

The first job was a stretch for his skills and didn't seem to inspire any interest from him. The second was a true business internship at a mid-sized construction company but would involve a long daily commute. The third was a fun, hospitality focused position in the city that allowed him to spend more time with his family. All three positions paid well, but he just couldn't see an obvious choice.

Using a long series of questions, I finally helped him to see that he really preferred the job that would work best with his family's schedule and provided a more fun, rather than educational, experience. Upon further discussion, I learned the internship with the business company in the suburbs was an open offer that he could accept now for the following summer. The research that we did looking into each company and understanding the benefits of each summer job paid off by helping him differentiate between the three roles.

It wasn't until he was able to see how each job would fill his needs for pay, location, convenience for his family, degree-related experience and, finally, fun did he really understand what to prioritize.

My final question to him in the process was to imagine each job offer was taken off the table by an email from that company. Which email would upset him the most to receive? By taking away each option, he could finally see where his passion and interest were most focused.

The next few chapters will help you determine where the best opportunities await you as you focus your personal brand on what you do best. This step involves research to examine where a need exists for your unique skills, personality traits, and life experiences.

Throughout my marketing career, I have learned research techniques that simply, methodically, and consistently determine what needs exist for products/services/workers and where to find these opportunities. Using this set of techniques will help you focus on outcomes that match your personal brand and save you time by preventing overthinking and indecision in the long run. In addition, these techniques work very well for individuals determining which activities to pursue in the short and long term for success.

"Destiny is no matter of chance. It is a matter of choice. It is not a thing to be waited for, it is a thing to be achieved."
– William Jennings Bryan

Finding opportunities

During Part Two of this book, we will use your newly discovered core list and self-awareness to find opportunities in work, life and play that are authentic and fulfilling for you.

Chapter 4 is designed to set you up for success. The exercises and topics discussed are meant to help you create a personal set of tools and strategies that will guide your search for a fulfilling career and life. Chapter 4 creates the framework to support all the work you will do later.

Chapter 5 is one of the most fun and creative chapters in this book. Most of the first half of the book consisted of remembering and recording observations and facts. The second half of the book is a strategic planning project. Chapter 5 allows you to dream about the possibilities that could be available to you.

Chapter 6 helps you research where your unique talents, skills, and personality traits are needed in a career, volunteer position, and/or hobby. Allow yourself adequate time for research and reflection.

It is highly recommended to complete each chapters' exercises before beginning the next as they build upon the prior work. If some exercises require more thinking time than others, that is okay. Do not rush the process of planning your future.

Strategically use your personal brand for your career and life so you can do what you love and love what you do.

Note: Each section contains a Lifestyle Track (focused on a hobby or lifestyle) as well as a Career Track (focused on jobs both paid and volunteer). Consider completing both tracks because a proper balance of work and play is healthy!

Chapter 4 Discover What You Love to Do: Finding Your Favorite Work and Life Activities

*"If your dreams do not scare you, they
are not big enough."*
– Ellen Johnson Sirleaf

Much of the work prior to this section required you to think hard about your life. This intense contemplation probably caused you to feel and experience a variety of emotions… not all of them good. Emotions and memories can have a way of lifting you up, but at the same time even the good ones can exhaust you.

When first working with a client, I ask a lot of questions that simply have to do with getting to know them better and making sure they are cared for during our time together and in the future.

Do you have a source of income to cover your basics needs?

What do you do for yourself?

How do you exercise, practice self-care, socialize, and have fun?

Many people are confused by the last part. What does any of that have to do with my business or career?

Taking care of your physical and mental health is vital to preparing yourself and your life for change. Even if that change is learning to be and share a more authentic and truer version of yourself.

The analogy I give is that of a company about to launch a brand-new product…maybe a shampoo, snack food, or sneaker. If the manufacturing is going great, but the finance department forgot to pay the electric bill for the factory... there is a problem. Or if the research and development department misplaced the data that provides the secret ingredient needed for the product... there is a problem. Or the legal department forgot to check the status of trademarks or patents ... there is a problem. Or the sales team missed a meeting with the largest big box store in the country... there is a problem. Or the ad agency and media buyers miscommunicated the length and number of commercials and videos needed for the media buy... there is a problem. I could go on for the length of this book on the number of people, departments, and processes that need to work well for a new product to get launched successfully. Millions of details need to be taken care of properly. A lot can go wrong. I am certain that you can think of a similar example in your industry.

Having been a part of multiple new product launch teams, a lot can go wrong. The percentage of new products that last past one year on the shelf is about as disappointing as the number of new restaurants that close within that first crucial year. So, what happens during that crucial first year that allows a product (or restaurant) to succeed? What is the secret ingredient or the magical quality that makes one product shine over all the others? Branding. And more importantly brand loyalty.

I was recently on a video call with a few colleagues and they were discussing how absolutely crushed they would be if their favorite restaurant closed. The call was during the first few months of the Covid-19 quarantine. It was at the end of a long workday and we were purposefully trying to find light-hearted conversation topics to raise our spirits after many weeks of uncertainty and sadness. The discussion included how they were buying takeout and gift cards for those restaurants, just to be certain each would stay open. That is brand loyalty in all its glory. And that is why having a strong personal brand is so important. Imagine what having fans of your personal brand can do for your business in any crises or economic downturn. Consider how a few fans with a few recommendations or referrals can change your bottom line.

Turning back to the new product analogy above, having all parts working is so important to the product's success. For you, all the individual parts of you that support your life need to work well, not exceptional, just well enough to give you the energy and stamina for the creativity and strength to grow.

"Growth is never by mere chance; it is the result of forces working together."
– James Cash Penney

Taking care of your physical and mental health is vital to preparing yourself and your life for change and growth. This care is especially important if that change is learning to be and share a more authentic, stronger, and truer version of yourself through your personal brand.

Growth requires energy and happiness. Happiness also requires effort.

"The belief that unhappiness is self-less and happiness is selfish is misguided. It is more selfless to act happy. It takes energy, generosity, and discipline to be unfailingly lighthearted, yet everyone takes the happy person for granted. No one is careful of his feelings or tries to keep his spirits high. He seems self-sufficient; he becomes a cushion for others. And because happiness seems unforced, that person usually gets no credit."
— Gretchen Rubin, The Happiness Project: Or Why I Spent a Year Trying to Sing in the Morning, Clean My Closets, Fight Right, Read Aristotle, and Generally Have More Fun

Growth requires energy.   Growth also requires motivation, lots of it, especially when it comes to growing your career.

So where can you find this motivation?

One way to find motivation is with my prescription for silliness with a dose of joy.

Joy Creators
When things get rocky and hope seems a pleasant but far away concept, the best we can do is look for the tiny sparks of joy that can get you through. A day or even a few minutes of pure joy can fill our tanks until we get to the next moment of happiness. The key is to create a stockpile of personal joy creators. Think of personal joy creators as a full and varied toolkit for transforming a troublesome or uninspiring moment into energy.

Note how I used the work "personal" joy creators. These tools are personal because the theoretical cabinet, suitcase, or backpack that contains them (or what I call the

Joy Creator Toolkit) is uniquely personalized for each of us.

What brings you joy and is in your Joy Creator Toolkit?

Start with your answers to the exercises in Chapter 2 and read the section on what to do if you get stuck.

Next, consider proven boosters of serotonin (your body's mood enhancing chemical): reading, listening to music, coloring, doing puzzles, playing games, painting, or having a conversation with a friend. Many of these recommendations have been proven to increase serotonin levels, which in turn combats depression. In fact, meditation, music, exercise, and sunlight have been proven in multiple studies to counteract depression and increase serotonin levels.

The key to making the Joy Creator Toolkit useful is to fill it with a variety of options. Each option should bring you joy or at least make you feel as if you have accomplished something creative or positive that gets you closer to your goals. When you need a lift in your mood or a little extra motivation, you can simply choose the one that works with your time, location, and resources. The small win of getting a task off your to do list is worth celebrating.

Here are a few examples of joy creators sorted by the approximate time it will take you to engage in the activity or item.

Short Joy Creators

Short joy creators should take between 1 and 5 minutes to do. Chew your favorite stick of gum. Listening to or, even better, dancing to your "happy" song. Watch a quick

YouTube video that makes you laugh. Laughter is infectious so share a good joke or clever story with a friend. Read an uplifting magazine or e-zine article. Send a positive text to lift up the spirits of a friend or family member. Do pushups, jumping jacks, or your favorite yoga pose. Have a cup of coffee, tea, or fruit-infused water. Take deep breaths. Spray your favorite scent or light a candle. Consider just listening to your heart, music, or a comedy radio channel.

Medium Joy Creators

Medium joy creators should take between 5 and 30 minutes to do. Take a hike. Walk outside, around a parking lot, or up and down flights of stairs. Call your best friend. Write an email or handwrite a thank you note to a friend. Listen to a podcast with a positive uplifting theme (A go-to podcast for joy is *Happier* with Gretchen Rubin and Elizabeth Craft). Play a game of solitaire or set a timer to play a video game for 15 minutes. Do a workout video. Prep your dinner or lunch for the next day. Chopping vegetables can be wonderfully cathartic and help you eat healthier. Play a musical instrument. Sort through the photos on your phone and get rid of any blurry or unflattering ones.

Long Joy Creators

Long Joy Creators can take anywhere from 1 hour to multiple days. These normally take a bit more planning to do, but longer activities are ideal for getting you out of a rut. Call a friend you haven't talked to in months. Go on a sabbatical to a new city. Read a book for fun. Garden. Take a hike, boat ride, or bike ride. Pack a picnic, even if

you are only eating on your front step. Attend a concert.
Check out free concerts or low-cost concerts from
community centers or schools. Go to a stand-up comedy
open mic night (trust me, they love having extra audience
members). Write in a journal. Attend a retreat, alumni
event, or friends' weekend away. Visit a museum. Cook a
meal from scratch while playing your favorite music. Do a
craft. Watch a classic film. The options are endless but
must be specific to what brings you joy.

Enjoy the process of creating a list of personal joy creators
for your Joy Creator Toolkit. Write them on index cards, a
poster for your workspace, a note on your phone, or a
calendar reminder that pops up every few days.   When
you feel sapped of energy, pull them out and pick one to
try.

Revisit the list every year or so to add or update what
brings you joy. Humans are complicated and what may
work this year could very well not work the next. Trying
new options also keeps the joy fresh and fun. Motivation is
always better and more effective with a touch of novelty.

Keep your Joy Creator Toolkit handy for when you need a
lift.

Cohesion in a Personal Brand with Disparate Parts
A colleague questioned me about how to bring the
disconnected parts of his personal brand into one cohesive
statement.   My initial answer was that we would have to
have a few more discussions to work through this concept.
Then I recalled that many of my clients had this exact
problem. When you try to combine vastly differing fields of

study or work, finding a method to see the patterns that underly seemingly different parts of a personal brand is key, especially during a career transition.

Normally, my clients and I take 3 months to really work through this exact issue in a deliberative process. For right now, consider the information you share with the world around you about yourself. Think about how that information is always presented in a contained package. You can only fit so much content into a sound bite, podcast, email, phone call, presentation, or LinkedIn profile. The key is understanding how to edit and control the authentic narrative to fit your "profersonal" (professional meets personal term coined by Jason Seiden) needs.

As an example, let me discuss my personal brand. My background in Research & Development means I have incredible patience and determination to spend lots of time and try many methods of research in order to help my clients understand exactly their precise target market without getting bored or frustrated. Years in a lab will do that for you. My volunteer work coaching kids for over a decade means that I have worked with, motivated, and helped grow almost every personality type out there. It also helps me to be non-judgmental and empathetic. Coaching has also taught me how to motivate my clients while helping them move beyond their stumbling blocks. One of my undergraduate degrees and years of writing for newsletters, newspapers, yearbooks, and more recently blogs, websites etc. combined with a mixed media side hustle creating sets and props for theater, means I have an endless supply of creativity.

The cohesion point of these experiences is that I am strategic, creative, and great at coaching people.

By creating a short list of key words that describe the authentic you, you will better understand how all the disparate parts of your life or work can coexist with each other.

Notice I didn't describe my personal brand as personal branding... because for me personal branding is a calling that allows me to use my gifts of strategy, creativity, and coaching but it is not my brand.

For your personal brand statement, revisit this statement when you are deciding on a new job, position, or taking up a new hobby. Consider how focusing on these statements will impact not only your life, but your relationships with others. Take it further to develop a strategy where you challenge yourself to try something new or learn something, so you can do each activity, job, or hobby better and with more joy. Act to make your life fulfilling!

"Change your life today. Don't gamble
on the future, act now, without delay."
– Simone de Beauvoir

Time management
With the rapid increase in the amount of information we are expected to process daily, How are we expected to find time for everything we need or want to do?

This quote from Karen Walker, a character on the long running television show *Will & Grace*, emphasizes the purpose of this section: with strategic planning you can find time for what you want to do.

"Sorry I'm late. I got here as soon as I wanted to." – Karen Walker

Focus on what you want to do and don't think about all the things you don't want to do and places you don't want to be… that's another book.

A few years ago, my business increased, my volunteer pro-bono work increased, and my commitments to my family and friends also increased. Not surprisingly, the amount of time in each day did not increase.

After quickly recovering from that shock, I did what any former scientist and MBA would do…research! Books, blog posts, infographics, webinars, and one-on-one conversations with experts yielded a solid list of strategies on how to gain more time… or, more truthfully, how to better schedule my time. Improving time management skills and productivity are worthwhile lifelong pursuits for me personally and perhaps for you as well.

Time Management = Increased Productivity

Productivity is directly related to how healthy you are physically, mentally, and emotionally. Take care of your body, mind, and soul, so you can take care of business. Automating your life by simplifying the regular decisions you make every day makes it easier for you to take care of business.

Here is my list of top tips and strategies for improving time management:

Time Management Tip 1: Just say NO!

As I said in Chapter 2, saying no is necessary to stay true to your authentic self. It is also is a key to time management. Don't add on more responsibilities that you don't want to do.

Admittedly, I used to be horrible at this one and still occasionally struggle. But using the knowledge of Greg McKeown from his book, *Essentialism: The Disciplined Pursuit of Less*, helped me focus on what is important… not just today, but with my long-term goals in mind.

> *"Time is a created thing. To say, 'I don't have time,' is like saying, 'I don't want to.'"* – Lao Tzu

We all have tasks we have to complete… "feed my family" and "pay bills or taxes." These are actions that will happen no matter what else you do and can often be outsourced via school lunch or autopay. Get creative on how to make your "must do" list as easy as possible. My "must do" list is a roof over our heads, food on the table, clothes on our backs and bills paid. These obviously need to occur, but anything that falls outside that list is up for discussion.

The hard part is learning HOW to say "no."

My favorite strategy for saying "no" is to keep a visual or mental list of what tasks I expect myself to accomplish. List every major task you can think of that you are responsible for or required to do this week/month/year. Use the Time Mapping exercise from Chapter 2. Circle the ones only you can do, delegate the rest if someone else can do them. For anything that falls somewhere in between do and delegate, ask yourself the following questions. Only keep the tasks that you can definitively answer YES to these two questions.

- Do I love and enjoy doing this?
- Does this task or activity directly help me towards one of my top three life goals?

Strategies for saying "no" include being honest, being direct, not hesitating, practicing saying "no," and not making unnecessary excuses. It is YOUR time. Be prepared to have to repeat the "no" over and over, especially from someone that is used to you saying yes.

My recommendation is to start out extremely polite and kind. Each time you must repeat the "no" make your response shorter and more to the point, until finally they will either get the message or enough time will pass that the request is no longer relevant or important.

Time Management Tip 2: Write it Down

"You may delay, but time will not."
– Benjamin Franklin

Planning your schedule is necessary if you have any chance of gaining time for what you want to do. Using the list of tasks and activities that take up your time, fill out your schedule for the next week in a planner.

A personal planner is effective *only* if it makes sense to you. I am a graduate of the Franklin Covey method, which is inspired by the productivity habits of Benjamin Franklin.

I use a modified version of the Franklin Covey planning method in a regular spiral bound single subject notebook that works for me (in a bright color so I don't lose it), combined with a Google Calendar, Calendly, Amazon's Alexa, my mobile phone and multiple large white boards in strategic locations. From all these different methods I may seem like an obsessive planner, but I'm not. Each thing I use to plan is based on the easiest way for me to find that particular planning information. Every person is unique and so should their method of planning. Find a notebook or planner that inspires you. Design or find an online or app-based planner that fits with your lifestyle, choice of technology, or work mode. There are many options out there. Finding one you believe in *and* will stick to will help you succeed.

Everyone has a different way of organizing their life and whatever method you use to write down your schedule should be specific to your needs and goals. The easiest, low cost, low tech version is to buy a spiral notebook. The spiral allows you to open it flat and fold back the cover in case you wish to use a book stand to make it easy to read.

At night before you go to bed or first thing in the morning, write the date at the top of the page and list out all the things you would like to accomplish that day. Include times and locations and with whom you will be doing the activity. Star or circle the one item that, if you accomplish it, will let you go to sleep that night satisfied that you did enough.

Cross out each task as you complete it. At the end of the day, go to the next page, write tomorrow's date at the top, and move all incomplete items from the current day's page over. Add additional items that need to be completed tomorrow. Again, star or circle the one task that will let you fall asleep satisfied tomorrow night. Don't forget to strategically cross off tasks that no longer need to be completed because the time has passed, goals have changed, or you have delegated the task to someone else.

To help you find your own planning technique, I included a few links on my blog Small Business, Big Brand (https://brandmarketing.home.blog/) under the How to Find More Time post. Work on always improving and revising your method to save you time and keep you organized.

Time Management Tip 3: Automate Your Life

"Those who make the worst use of their time are the first to complain of its brevity." – Jean de La Bruyère

Automate as many areas of your regular daily life. This will reduce decision time and effort on everyday tasks that do not require your high level creative and problem-solving skills. Save those skills for when you truly need them!

In his book, *The Power of Habit*, Charles Duhigg advocates for simplifying your decision-making to gain more time for your brain to work on more complex problems. I would also add that by simplifying your decision-making, you will gain time that would otherwise have been wasted on indecision. The most important part of automating your life is to do it one small step at a time. If you try to change too many habits at once, you will most likely get frustrated and stop.

Examples of how to automate your life by simplifying habits include:

Automating Bill Payment

Autopay is your friend, so is paperless billing. Every time you pick up a piece of mail you need to think about shredding, recycling, responding, and filing. Why not just have that paperless and autopay bill get filed in your digital storage for you to regularly look over once a week or once a month?

Clothing Organization

Do you have set uniforms for all of the regularly occurring activities on your calendar? Look at your schedule for the next two weeks. List what you would wear at each one. Consider organizing your closet and drawers by activity and create your own list of categories.

Category examples: Presentations and Corporate Meetings, Work at the Office, Work from Home, Networking Events, Exercise Clothes, Weekend Time with Friends, Special Occasion, Attending Sporting Events/Theater, Travel Clothes, Vacation Clothes.

My list includes: Board Meetings, Presentations, Networking Events and Client Meetings, Workout Clothes, Clothes to Wear to My Kids Sporting Events or While Coaching, Writing/Working from Home Clothes, Formal Wear: Cocktail and Black Tie, Airplane/Travel Clothes.

Consider what the uniform for each category needs to accomplish. Do you need to look professional? Do you need to be comfortable? Do you need to be active? Will you have to change quickly due to timing? Will the outfit travel well? What shoes and accessories will match each outfit?

If you start each day already knowing which category you need, you won't waste as much time worrying about what to wear because the options will be simplified.

Plan Your Meals

Consider how you fuel your body. Spending a few minutes each week meal-planning saves money and time. If you need inspiration, consult with a registered dietician/nutritionist or a food-planning book. My favorite to recommend is *The Total Body Diet* by Vicki Shanta Retelny. The book covers a complete makeover based on science for your diet and eating habits. Find a food plan that works for your lifestyle and health needs.

Weekly meal-planning strategy:

- Take Stock. Look at what you currently have in your pantry, refrigerator, and freezer.

- Check your Schedule. Decide which meals you will cook and eat at home, which you will pack to eat elsewhere, and which you will eat out at a restaurant or event.

- Make a List. For the meals you will prepare, make a shopping list of ingredients based on recipes of what you already have at home. Use what is in your kitchen to inspire the menu. Keep a running list of staple items you always buy on your virtual assistant shopping list or notes section of your smartphone. Or print out a list of everything you would buy separated by grocery department and circle this week's list. The ultimate time saver is to use a delivery service or a click-and-shop service, where you shop online and send a text when you arrive at the store for a store clerk to bring the shopping list of food directly to the trunk of your car.

- Prep ahead. Decide what ingredients you can prepare ahead of time (chop vegetables and proteins, make bread, soak legumes, or precook rice, quinoa, or pasta, etc.) Try to do as much of the prep work in a single time period at the beginning of the week so you have more time during the week.

- BYOB. If you are trying to start a business or save for a fabulous vacation, this is a budget area that is easy to cut back on, but only if you plan. Take coffee with you ($1) instead of buying it on the road ($4).

- Limit your choices. Have the same thing for breakfast everyday… or most days. Or limit your breakfast and lunch choices to 2-3. Less choices means less time deciding and fewer ingredients to purchase.

Schedule Your Workout Like a Meeting

Plan and schedule your workouts just as you would a business meeting. Maintaining a healthy body and brain helps you perform at your highest potential. Search the

Internet for the benefits of exercise and an unending list of sources pops up.

Signing up for a specific class each week or working with a personal trainer to develop a few workout routines will help keep you focused. Add in a workout partner or friend in real life or virtually for accountability.

I have four unique workout routines I rotate between. They are simple and cover all of my needs across cardio, strength training, range of motion, and stretching. I also have them printed out to carry with me in my gym bag and have them posted in my office. A few times a year I look over the routines and consult with a trainer on how to up the intensity or focus on different goals, like recovering from an injury, fitting into my clothes better, training for bike ride in a National Park, or preparing for a fundraising walk/run.

Keeping the exercise type listed in your planner each day helps you look forward to it, pack proper clothing/equipment, and maintain an interesting mix without having to think too hard. Make sure to include one workout that is easy to do on the road or during vacation and requires little or no special equipment. Reduce excuses on why not to work out and always remember, every little bit helps. Start small. A 10-minute walk around your office parking lot at lunch or around your neighborhood after dinner is better than nothing.

Create a Sleep Routine

Sleep is so important. To continuously perform at a high level at work and in life, getting enough sleep is vital. If you schedule a routine for bedtime, you will more likely be able to keep those precious hours of rest safe.

In his infographic titled, "11 ways to improve productivity without coffee," Chris Jager offers some great ideas on how to improve productivity without a huge influx in caffeine.

Habit 6 in this extremely useful infographic explains the optimal amount of sleep to improve your productivity.

Managing your time wisely will open up more time to work on improving your future. Combining a strong list of self-care routines with time management and a reduction in decision making will inevitably lead to a stronger, healthier and more successful you.

Prioritization Hacks

A key to prioritizing is understanding your goals.

To figure out your top three goals, imagine you have less than a year to live. What are the three things that you really want to do with your time? Then think more broadly and make a bucket list of 25 actions and note which ones are the most important to you.

Or, in a less morbid way of thinking, imagine that you won the lottery and are obligated to keep it a secret to the world for one year at which time you will receive the money. In that time, what would you do with your current life and spending limits?

Consider the tasks or responsibilities that bring you the most stress and anxiety. Ask yourself, is this a commitment I need to do now, but can work towards removing from my life in the next three months? Set a date on your calendar for three months from now and actively work to offload anything you do not want to do anymore.

> *"You can have it all. Just not all at once."*
> – Oprah Winfrey

A final way to learn and name your top priorities is align it with your personal brand. Ask yourself, does this activity or responsibility authentically represent my personal brand?

Which activities you prioritize may even surprise you. But they should at a minimum help guide your decisions about how you spend your time going forward.

Chapter 4 Exercises

Prioritizing your time

Sometimes it is hard to see on a day-to-day basis what to prioritize... putting out fires or long-term goals. Take some time to let yourself look at your life from a prioritization perspective. You are not getting graded or evaluated, so feel free to be honest and do this exercise at the speed you feel comfortable.

This exercise is about prioritizing what not only brings you joy, but also fulfillment. Do not worry about what you must do or are committed to do. Many obligations can be removed, outsourced, or delegated to someone else. It may take a lot of time, but the real goal of this exercise is to learn what you truly want to keep doing.

Look at all the lists you have created on how you spend your time and evaluate each role, responsibility, and activity.

- ♥ Put a heart next to the three that you want to do every week for the next year. Don't be reasonable or think too hard about which ones you will choose. Imagine money and time and travel are not limitations.
- ☐ Put a box around the one thing you must do to support yourself and your family or the one/two you need to do to honor a commitment. Imagine all other commitments would no longer be obligations. Choose only one or two at most.
- ∗ Put a star next to the one that gives you the most pride and joy that you have not marked with a heart or boxed already.

List the 5 activities, roles, obligations, and hobbies you marked above.

Which ones are you passionate about, fulfilled by, and/or inspired by to live your life more completely?

1.

2.

3.

4.

5.

To help with this exercise, you may need to step back or change your routine a bit to think more clearly about how to prioritize the different parts of your life. If you are still having trouble, reread the prioritization hacks at the beginning of the chapter.

Create your Personal Brand
Now it is your turn to tell your own story.

"One of the most courageous things you can do is identify yourself, know who you are, what you believe in and where you want to go."
– Sheila Murray Bethel

The previous exercises were meant to help you understand yourself better. Starting with this exercise, you will begin creating the story that you will share and tell the world when you are ready. Don't hold back. Be brave. Be authentic. Speak truthfully and with passion. Your story is important and uniquely yours. Be strong in telling it.

Personal Brand Statement

Fill in the blanks below with your answers from all of the exercises you have completed.

Personal Brand for _____ (your name)

I am known for being really good at _____
(skill), _____(talent)
and _____(skill/or/talent).

My friends and coworkers know they can expect me to always be _____,
_____ and
_____(personality traits).

I am passionate about ....

I feel inspired when I ....

I feel fulfilled when I ....

113

"Step out of the history that is holding you back. Step into the new story you are willing to create." – Oprah Winfrey

Finding Your Happy Place

This exercise is a simple visualization to help you create a memory tool that will calm you and comfort you when you are feeling stressed or uncertain. It is one of my Joy Creators and I use it with the teams I coach during competitions and practices to help them stay calm, focused, and having fun.

Close your eyes (well, read the next two paragraphs first and then close your eyes).

Think of a time in which you remember being filled with joy and happiness. Look around and see the scenery around you, noticing small details like the temperature of the air or the color of flowers or buildings or objects nearby. Remember what it smelled like... fresh and optimistic or warm and comforting or sharp and invigorating. Listen. Remember what you heard, music or laughter or the beat of a train or the splash of water. Go back to temperature and remember how your skin felt. What clothes were you wearing? See the ground beneath you. Focus finally on what action you were doing at the time. Remember the rhythm of your motions. If you were sitting or lying still at the time, remember the rhythm of your breathing and your heart beating. Or the way your eyes blinked.

Take a deep breath and feel the joy you felt at the time. Repeat the deep breath and focus on the feeling of joy. Then pause, take a mental snapshot of all the feelings and images, and sounds and smells that you felt at that exact moment.

Whenever you need a lift from a troubling moment to get to the next moment, take a deep breath, and remember this memory. That is how you find your Happy Place.

A Final Thought about Time

Look over the last few pages about work, volunteer work, hobbies, and commitments. Read through the topics at the end of this chapter about how to decide how to spend your time and when to unsubscribe or say No. Think carefully and openly without judgement about each role you have and how they interact and affect each other both positively and negatively. Giving up one will likely make the others better.

Chapter 5 Create Your Future: Dare to Dream

"Every great dream begins with a
dreamer. Always remember, you have
within you the strength, the patience, and
the passion to reach for the stars to
change the world." – Harriet Tubman

For this chapter, you are invited to describe your dreams for an ideal future. The exercises help you list the specific environments and circumstances that you find most appealing. Later, you will be able to match these details with jobs and roles that fit your unique personal brand. Writing down and actively think about details will help you to recognize which opportunities to take when they come your way.

One of the most important topics discussed in this section of the book is how to increase creativity. During the exercises in this chapter, you will need as much creativity and open mindedness as possible. The ability to think outside the box and come up with unusual or wildly surprising ideas is so very important.

Be aware that the exercises in this chapter may take a few days or weeks as the creative process needs time to unconsciously make connections and see patterns that, at first glance, may not make sense.

"There are no great limits to growth because there are no limits of human intelligence, imagination, and wonder."
– Ronald Reagan

If you have a highly creative person in your life – a colleague, friend, mentor, or confidant – this may be the point to ask them to join you for a while on your journey. Their help brainstorming will allow you to see beyond your view to more opportunities. Explain that you don't need them to do a lot of work, simply to act as a sounding board and brainstorming partner. You need someone that knows you personally to bounce ideas off. Remind them (and yourself) that there are no bad ideas. And even the most unexpected or outlandish thoughts can generate the desired result. The time for editing or disposing of ideas is later, not now.

Consider taking your highly creative friend out for coffee or doing a virtual tea-time over video conference. Long car, train, or plane rides also offer wonderful uninterrupted and low pressure time for creative discussions. Ask them to join you fishing, hiking, shopping, or walking to allow for a natural and comfortable amount of time to let both of your minds wander and open to the possibilities.

The outside perspective from someone who cares about you will give you a much-needed fresh look at who you are after many exercises done on your own.

And, of course, don't forget to thank them for collaborating with you on this journey. Don't be afraid to let them know – at least in a broad sense – what your overall goal of working on your personal brand will help you achieve. They will feel invested in helping you reach the goal and may become your biggest cheerleader and accountability coach during the process. These two great team member roles will help you reach your goals! Finally, at the end of the process, when you start taking action, you will already have a wise advisor with a background in the situation to guide your decisions.

Don't be surprised if they ask for your help in return as they tackle one of their personal dilemmas. Seeing someone work for change and improvements in their lives inspires others to do the same.

Again, remember that this is a process that may take more time than the previous sections as it involves ruminating over the possibilities. Dream about the future... your future. Don't be afraid to have fun. Be fearless! Dream without limits.

Achieving Duel Goals to Find a Niche and Fill a Need
Working with my clients, I always discuss two specific needs that must be fulfilled in any career or life choice.

You need (1) the work that feeds you and (2) the work that feeds your soul.

Sometimes you choose one over the other, but both must be present. If you are lucky, they will overlap or even exist in one work position.

Feeding you simply means can you put bread on your table, a roof over your head, and clothes on your back?

Basically, a paycheck to pay for your bare minimum living expenses.

Feeding your soul is more complicated. Food for the soul – in this situation – is the work that gets you out of bed in the morning. The work that you have pride in. Often it may be the volunteer work or hobby or side hustle beyond your full-time job.

One of the best ways to feed your soul is to try to make the world a better place. To make a difference using your abilities, skills, talents, and experiences. Before going further, think about how you personally can make a difference. This may not lead to a role or responsibility immediately, but perhaps in a few years your life will open to allow you to contribute to society in a new way.

> *"Everyone has a purpose in life and a unique talent to give to others. And when we blend this unique talent with service to others, we experience the ecstasy and exultation of our spirit, which is the ultimate goal of all goals."*
> *– Kallam Anji Reddy*

The Power of Daydreams

Remember in kindergarten how your teacher asked everyone to share what they wanted to be when they grew up? That may have been your very first career daydream.

A daydream is allowing your mind to wander wherever you want it to go while you are awake. Daydreaming is the ability to imagine your life as you wish it could be. Daydreaming is pretending to do something completely in your imagination. The most important part of daydreaming is the complete lack of boundaries and limitations. In your daydreams, you can be anyone you want to be, do anything you want to do, and go anywhere you want to go.

As children, both imagination and playing pretend are crucial to growth and development both individually and socially.

In his *Psychology Today* article entitled, "The Need for Pretend Play in Child Development," Scott Barry Kaufman cites several psychology research studies that uphold the theory of how important imaginative play is to cognitive and human development.

As we grow older, the ability to daydream is almost forgotten in the pragmatic day to day of adult life.

My challenge to you is to never stop daydreaming.

The power of daydreams is that they are open, unlimited spaces to creatively build the life we want even if it is impossible. The power of daydreams is the ability to make the impossible less so when we take a risk-free walk through our own daydreams.

In sports, this risk-free walk is called visualization. For over a decade, I have had the privilege of coaching kids on soccer, baseball, softball, track, and cross-country teams. And, more recently, I have been coaching a middle school robotics team. Games, meets, and competitions for kids can be nerve wrecking and intense. My main jobs as a coach are to inspire, teach, encourage, and, most importantly, help the team learn how to deal with stress, nervousness, and self-doubt.

Before a particularly intense part of competition, I ask my team to relax and visualize a calm scene, normally somewhere in nature that they love. The paragraph below is an example of guided visualization. It can be done on your own as a form of meditation or visualization. And, yes, it works for business presentations or job interviews as well.

Guided Visualization Meditation

Imagine a beach or a path through the woods that meanders beside a stream. See the trees and flowers around you. Imagine the wind gently blowing softly through the trees. Birds singing and chirping quietly overhead. Imagine it is not too hot nor too cold. Now take a deep breath. Switch your focus to you here in the competition, on the field, in the game, in the office. Imagine you are doing what you have practiced and everything you do is exactly as you have planned. Every action is done perfectly and feels effortless. You are doing great. See yourself succeeding. Imagine you are achieving the goal you set out to accomplish. Now take a deep breath. Smile and open your eyes to the world around you.

Daydreaming for Success

A simple exercise that does not take more than a few minutes can have astronomically wonderful effects on the self-esteem of a student athlete or team member. By walking the team through the guided visualization (essentially a daydream) I gave each of them the opportunity to see what is possible, to give hope, encouragement and to help them believe in themselves.

Consider your daydreams a source for what could be possible. Daydreams are a source of motivation and encouragement from within to create a desire to stretch yourself a little beyond your comfort zone. By stretching yourself even a small amount, you will find the energy to be more, do more, and try that one extra time that helps you reach your goal.

Achieving your goals is a result of encouragement, hope, motivation, and inspiration. All of which are supported and strengthened through the power of daydreams.

Improving Creativity

In one of the exercises below you will be asked to create your dream job. This is not an easy task if your creativity is blocked. Creativity is a muscle that needs to be stretched and strengthened. A creativity workout allows you to strengthen your creative muscles so you can use them when needed for a work or personal project.

In *The 12 Secrets of Highly Creative Women*, author Gail McMeekin interviewed forty-five women to better understand the source and experience of their creativity. The book is intended to act as a creativity mentor to help others find, grow, and express their creativity. Ms. McMeekin asserts that everyone can be creative. "Creativity is not just for 'talented geniuses'. Creativity is a tool we can all access and utilize. It doesn't matter if you've never picked up a pen or can't draw a straight line or flunked out of music class, you have a creative self just waiting to be awakened or amplified." Take her words to heart and know you are creative.

As a writer, brand marketer, and content creator, I need a continuous source of creativity to create messaging that will resonate with the intended audience. To keep the stream of creativity flowing, I try to extend my creative output beyond simply writing to visual media, and other forms of art.

One of my favorite creative projects each year is to design sets for a local school musical performance. Each project starts with an inspiration session that can last weeks before the actual set is drawn, and construction begins. After I have compiled a stack of drawings and notes, I sit down with the director, event planner, or building team and discuss the limitations of the stage, set pieces and whatever other parameters will control the design. Taking the time to fill my mind and sketch book with ideas allows me to design with depth and an attention to detail. After all, the goal is to surprise and delight with a scene that not only enhances the performance, but transports the audience to a whole, new world.

"Flood your life with ideas from many sources. Creativity needs to be exercised like a muscle." – Brian Tracy

My personal process for getting inspired has evolved over the years, but a few specific sources have remained. Many of the techniques I use can also help you become more creative

Try one of these creativity tips this week to see if it inspires creativity in you.

Creativity Tip 1: Go see, stream, or rent a movie. Hollywood has provided us with a lifetime of visual inspiration. Watch a period piece to see how fabric and knickknacks have changed over the years. Use the brilliance of CGI to imagine color and size combinations that will make your design memorable. Immerse yourself in the story to understand what elements are expected. For example, I reluctantly forced myself to sit through a horror movie in preparation for a haunted house design and was shocked at how much it helped me with details like lighting, staging, costumes, and props.

Creativity Tip 2: Break out the crayons and coloring books. The seemingly simplistic design of coloring books focuses the person coloring on lines, angles, and curves. Coloring books have evolved from a time spender for children into a vast industry of books designed to help calm and inspire adults. Coloring books are a great jumping off point for big picture design. The act of coloring is a quiet yet active form of mindfulness. Not that you couldn't let your mind wander while coloring, but it does allow for a removal of all distraction as you focus on filling in a shape with color. Spending a few minutes coloring has been shown to relax adults, allowing their minds to open and think tangentially about a situation, problem, or design. Another spin is to create or read comic books or cartoons. Both offer clean, efficient images that move a story forward. The carefully curated visual and text of each can inspire creativity.

Creativity Tip 3: Take a hike. Look for art and architecture.

Take a walk around a city. Look at the statues including their bases. Examine fences, bridges, walls, and buildings. Look at details like trim and windows to see layers of pattern. Walk in nature. Note the way water changes color. Compare the texture of different bark, leaves, and stones.   Watch how leaves on a tree move in the wind.

Creativity Tip 4: Grab your passport.

Ok, not literally. Go to Netflix, Amazon, a library, thrift store or bookstore and find travel films, books, and shows. Seeing somewhere far away can open your eyes to create a mind-blowing space. I especially love House Hunters International, episodes of the short-lived TV series *Better Late than Never*, the Rick Steves' travel videos, tour apps like teletour and anything in the *Visions* travel series. These companies take a lot of time to get lighting, storytelling and composition perfect. In addition, the ability to send video via apps like *Marco Polo* can allow you to share or experience far off travels with your wanderlust friends from the comfort of your home.

Being creative is a process that requires inspiration and a muse.

Find yours by seeking out what inspires you… art, nature, architecture, food, music, performance.

Be patient. Practice being creative every day and inspiration will strike!

How to Thrive During a Crisis

In everyone's business and personal life, there inevitably comes crises. Chaos. A complete overturning of your life beyond your control. A crises could be the loss of a job, collapse of an industry, demotion or a public relations nightmare. It could be the onset of disease, illness, or injury. Crisis can come in the form of a hurricane, tornado, flood, pandemic, or fire.

At these times, the best parts of people, communities, and companies are given the opportunity to shine and truly make a difference.

But this only happens if they choose to stay strong, engage, and step up to the challenge.

Simply going by the disaster playbook—the what-if scenarios and following the pretend drills—is not enough. It is a start, but not enough to thrive. Thriving during a crisis requires you to call upon your skills, innovative creativity, and love/empathy for our fellow humans. For the people we share this planet with, to engage and thrive during a crisis means pulling from our reserves of both energy and strategic thinking.

Historically, the signs of a great leader during crises are focused on three main responses: communication, instilling hope, and seeking help from the experts. Great leaders during a crisis do all three. For you, choosing to step up during a crisis requires you to do all three as well.

So how do you thrive during a crisis?

Crisis Response Tip 1: Communication
The first priority is to openly, authentically communicate an awareness of the crises. Secondly, research and share the limitations, constraints, and issues. Finally, communicate a willingness to work through it. You will prove you are ready to solve the crisis or at least survive and move on from it.

Crisis Response Tip 2: Instill Hope
By practicing exceptional communication, including valuable listening skills to the correct parties, you will convey through your words a message of resilience, hope, character, strength, and trust. The optimistic assurance, that no matter what—we can and will work through this—is vital to showing that you have the ability and willingness to step up to make the situation better.

Crisis Response Tip 3: Seeking Help
To thrive during a crisis requires the honesty to humbly ask for help. We are not silos or islands. We are not separated from the rest of the world. We need to actively be a part of society, but it also means we need to reach out when something is beyond us. A true leader can only be successful by admitting weakness and limitation. A true leader seeks help strategically and intelligently when they need it.

Go back to the first response of a great leader in crises: Communication. Clearly communicate all of the above. Living through a crisis is both overwhelming and frightening. After the initial shock, we are given the opportunity to choose to make life better for ourselves and others, but only if we choose to engage and meet the crisis head on.

Chapter 5 Exercises

The exercises below will help you describe opportunities that attract you and make the most of your personal brand. By listing the career and life opportunities that you are looking for, you will know when to go after or accept the opportunity when it becomes available.

As a review, start with going over your personal brand from the perspective of what motivates you and what are your true passions. Then, consider all aspects of potential opportunities and use your creativity and knowledge to further define what appeals to you and fits with your personal brand.

Think about the process of looking for a new home or apartment. A lot of factors need to be considered: location, cost, number of bedrooms/bathrooms, kitchen, décor, monthly maintenance fees, parking or public transportation, elevator or stairs, outdoor space, amenities, close to work/family/school, and stores nearby. Without thinking about and naming your ideal choices ahead of time, the process of choosing a place to live is overwhelming.

The same applies to finding a career or job. With careful thought and clearly stating your ideal choices, you are more likely to find the career you want and the one that is a great fit for your life.

Passionately choose what will make an amazing work opportunity for you.

Be specific.

Understand that what you need in an ideal work situation is unique to you and extremely important to define. You may not get everything you want in a perfect job, but without writing it down and asking yourself what you want, you can't expect to find it or get it.

"If you want to discover the true character of a person, you have only to observe what they are passionate about."
– Shannon L. Alder

Passion & Strength

Find your passion.

By this point, you have spent a lot of time learning what drives you and helps you make decisions… in a sense what makes you tick and gets you excited. That drive and motivation come from passion. When thinking about where you want to go and what you want to do, start first with your passions.

Passion is defined as "an intense desire or enthusiasm for something."

Ask yourself the following questions:

What am I deeply passionate about?

What topics do I love thinking, talking, learning, and reading about?

Think of the subjects you spend the most enjoyable time online or in print researching via video or articles.

Think about the conversations you love having during cocktail parties or conferences.

"Working hard for something we don't care about is called stressed; working hard for something we love is called passion." – Simon Sinek

Think about how the subjects you are most passionate about relate to your current or future career. Consider how the best part of your work could become the majority of your work.

By thinking deeply about what you are passionate about from a conversational level to how you want to spend your time, you can better understand the link between finding your passions and fulfilling work.

Know Your Strengths

You have already listed talents and skills that you know you are good at. List these and focus on the ones that directly tie into what you are passionate about.

Strengths are defined as "an asset of special worth or utility."

Ask yourself the following question:

What talents/skills do I excel at, have I mastered, or are easy and natural for me?

Again, start with the lists from Chapter 2 to create a list of strengths.

> *"The secret of joy in work is contained in one word – excellence. To know how to do something well is to enjoy it."*
> *– Pearl Buck*

Often there is an alignment between what we are passionate about and what we are good at. Our strengths tend to be the starting point for our passions.

Consider listing your strengths in one column and your passions in another column. Draw lines linking each strength to one or more passions.

See where you create the largest number of connections and start there. That is where you are likely to find a job, career, or hobby that will bring you the most fulfillment.

List Your Requirements & Non-Negotiables

Everyone has certain non-negotiables.

This is not a long list of items but only those two to three things that must be in place in order to feel like you have made the correct choice. Think about what those are for you.

Your non-negotiables may be a certain starting salary, location, great benefits, close to your family, specific job title, easy commute, number of vacation days, or autonomy in projects. Consider what one or two details would make compromising on other aspects of the job much easier. Inevitably you will have to compromise with some aspect of the perfect role. It is empowering to know ahead of time where you can accept compromise and where you are willing to wait until the right opportunity comes along.

This list of non-negotiables are the items you mention first when asked what type of job you are looking for during discussions with a headhunter, career coach, or job search platform. Be open, honest, and vocal and be prepared to push back when they attempt to sway you from what you consider important.

Having the non-negotiables front and center during your job hunt is absolutely necessary. The process of using your personal brand to find a fulfilling job or career depends on meeting your own unique criteria.

Part of decision-making is having standards or prerequisites to eliminate choices that will not fit the needs of the situation. Using a short – emphasis on short – list of your non-negotiables will help narrow down the list of options to a more manageable decision.

Non-negotiables will often align with your basic needs in a work situation. This is to be expected as demonstrated in Maslow's hierarchy of needs.

Saul McLeod, in an article from *Simply Psychology*, states "Needs lower down in the hierarchy must be satisfied before individuals can attend to needs higher up."

Therefore, higher level needs like fulfillment and reaching one's potential will be secondary in nature to basic needs of survival including food, shelter, and safety.

Write your list of non-negotiables and then see how it compares to your current and previous work roles. How many times have you had to compromise when you didn't want to? It is likely that a forced compromise on one or more of your non-negotiables was the underlying cause behind you leaving the last job you had.

Now you have the opportunity to choose your future during this creative, dream phase of job seeking. Hold tight to your non-negotiables. What will you fight for to find fulfillment?

Discover Your Motivators

Motivation is unique for every person and every situation. What may have motivated you to finish one project or task will not necessarily work for all projects or tasks. Focus on what has consistently motivated you in a work or project environment and hopefully across many teams or organizations. Look for the patterns that motivated you to follow a project through to completion.

Types of motivation include working for the greater good, clear and obvious return on investment, visual or tangible evidence of success in the form of a product or content, the joy of being in "flow" during work, a financial or beneficial award at the completion of the project or task, and the pleasure of working alongside a great team or leader.

Now consider the type of role that you would likely be considered for and what motivations go along with those roles. If you need a huge financial incentive, then look for careers that have high paychecks or bonuses. If you need to be doing something for the greater good, consider a non-profit or services related industry. If you love the glamor of the stage or enjoy the rush of an audience and the energy of live applause, consider roles that offer you time in front of an audience or interacting with a lot of people. If you love a certain type of manager or leader in an organization, make sure questions about teams and leadership are on your job interview list of questions for the person interviewing you.

To keep you focused, ask yourself the following questions about motivation:

> What do I need my future career or position to provide for me?

> What part of this work or hobby will bring me joy and fulfillment?

> What list of boxes must be checked for you to want to do this?

The answers to these questions will help you determine if a role or organization is right for you and may lead you in the direction of a new or unexplored industry.

> *"I can't change the direction of the wind, but I can adjust my sails to always reach my destination." – Jimmy Dean*

Work Environment

*"Make your physical surroundings as
beautiful as possible."*
– Alexandra Stoddard

Where we work can drastically change how well we work
and our job satisfaction. The plethora of co-working
spaces rapidly opening speaks to the need for inspiring
spaces. The time, attention, and financial investment
corporations put into designing headquarters that inspire or
intimidate also indicates the importance that physical
space has to growing and running a successful business.

As we move towards a gig economy, the need for
comfortable at-home, co-working, or shared workspace will
grow.

What I find fascinating is that both traditional corporate
offices as well as co-working spaces are using research
and data to alter work environments to improve not only
productivity (which they have been doing since the 1800s),
but also to increase workforce retention. Fully stocked
kitchens, gyms, standing or treadmill desks, community
building events, and other perks are just a few ways
companies/co-working spaces are trying to attract and
keep workers happy and productive.

Think about where you want to work. Describing your ideal
work-from-home office is a great place to start as
opportunities for employees to work partly (or entirely) from
home increase.

Since this was written during the pandemic of 2020, I frequently ran into evidence that at-home offices across the globe were receiving upgrades.

To prepare for a fall semester of multiple kids doing remote learning, we headed as a family to IKEA to buy more desks (wearing masks, of course). The stock of small desks was completely depleted mid-summer. It was disappointing and frustrating to not have any options.

At first, I was confused because the decision for most schools to continue remote learning for that area was rather recent. Then my husband pointed out the obvious connection between everyone that could work from home suddenly as of March 2020 being forced to work from home. Of course, there was a desk shortage!

It did make me wonder about how else the pandemic affected office, big box, and furniture stores. What other home office supplies ran low during the pandemic? How long until the shelves were replenished? What will happen to the office buildings or retail spaces that don't open back up? There was a lot to think about with regard to the major shifts in the workplace going forward. During a webinar on the future of human resources, one expert panelist described the pandemic shifts in workplace as moving the work/life balance forward by 10 years. It seems like work-from-home will continue.

I have worked from home for over a decade, but most people have not had or wanted that opportunity. Creating a work-from-home office that works for you requires creativity and a well thought out design. Consider hiring a professional organizer or architect to think creatively about reworking your space. If it helps increase your productivity, the expense will be worth it in the long run. Not everyone has the option to work from home, so if this does not apply to you, do not worry. Focus on where you would want to work in the future.

"Love yourself enough to create an environment in your life that is conducive to the nourishment of your personal growth. Allow yourself to let go of the people, thoughts, and situations that poison your well-being. Cultivate a vibrant surrounding and commit yourself to making choices that will help you release the greatest expression of your unique beauty and purpose." – Steve Maraboli.

Where Do You Want to Work

List where you find yourself the most productive... office, home, shared office, co-working space, outside, in the field... be specific and descriptive.

List everything from the type of desk or work surface, to the tools and office supplies you need.

At the end of every summer, parents and students rush to purchase school supplies. One of my clients described the utter joy of being able to pick out the notebooks, pens, and markers that would make school much more fun.

Kit Yarrow, Ph.D., a psychologist whose research focused on consumer behavior described the importance of Back-to-School shopping in her 2018 *Psychology Today* article, "Back-to-School Shopping: It Goes Deeper Than You Think." "Back-to-school shopping is about much more than the thrill of finding the perfect new backpack, it's emotional preparation." "But the reason that both parents and kids have described this as richly satisfying to me is because that process of imagining and discussing the future is exactly the psychological preparation everyone needs as kids transition from one grade to the next or leave home for the first time."

This form of supply shopping should also be done when you are starting a new job. Acknowledging the change with a new set of pens or a new pair of shoes seems trivial until you realize that the purchase helps ease and mark the importance of the transition.

Determining the best work environment also includes – like the real estate mantra – location, location, location.

Describe the ideal location (rural, urban, suburban, city, street, neighborhood) and commute (long or short, public transportation, bike, walk, drive, none!).

Is it located near a specific store, restaurant, school, or gym?

What type of windows and lighting are important to you?

John Rampton in his article, "10 Ways to Create a More Productive Work Environment" in *Entrepreneur*, emphasizes specific ways to change work environments for the better. "Let in as much natural light as possible. Research from the National Renewable Energy Laboratory found that those persons working in natural lighting stayed on-task for 15 percent longer than who worked in artificial lighting only." "Place plants throughout the office and allow your team to decorate their areas and personal spaces as they like."

List the lighting, furniture, plants, decorations, or interior design that you are most attracted to and inspired by.

The people who work with you are an integral part of the environment where you work. Consider any changes that may need to occur to optimize your work environment by changing who you spend time with. This can be as simple as actively seeking projects with people who inspire you or taking an open desk near someone that keeps you productive and motivated.

Describe the team of individuals you will be in contact with throughout the day both in person and virtually via phone, computer, or video call.

"Choose to focus your time, energy and conversation around people who inspire you, support you and help you to grow you into your happiest, strongest, wisest self." – Karen Salmansohn

This exercise is intended to help you thrive. By focusing on an environment that will cater to your productivity and aesthetic needs, you will gain an immediate shortcut to a higher level of performance, before even starting the job.

List a summary of your preferences from the lists above.

(Complete – if applicable and possible -for an outside-the-home and work-from-home option. Just in case.)

- Physical description
- Location

- Human Factor/Co-workers

- Technology or other tools you need

- Office Perks

Focus on what is the most important to you and circle three items from your work-space wish lists above that you can't live without.

Finding a Perfect Match

"Efforts and courage are not enough
without purpose and direction."
– John F. Kennedy

The purpose of this exercise is to help you use online search tools to find jobs, industries, or hobbies that you may not be aware of or have not considered before. Think of this exercise as answering a barrage of multiple-choice questions for career software designed to show high school students what careers they are most likely to enjoy or will succeed in.

Start by listing jobs and/or hobbies – real or invented – for which you would be a great candidate. Search for open positions in real companies and save the descriptions and requirements of candidates in a file for future use.

Next look back at your skills from the beginning of the book and insert them into a job hunt site. What job openings does the site suggest for you?

Consider what jobs career counselors, mentors, colleagues, and friends have suggested that would be a good fit for you.

IMPORTANT: For this exercise, be open minded and don't consider limitations or restrictions.

Consider your favorite jobs from your past work experience and pretend you are offered a promotion to a higher level of responsibility or an even more enjoyable description of responsibilities. Consider what a step up would look like if you moved to the top company in your industry or even a competitor. Step up your opportunities to the next level. Dream big.

Summarize all the job descriptions or roles into one list from the above searches.

After each position, briefly list what makes you a good candidate for the job or perfect to start/continue this hobby.

For anyone looking to find a new hobby or not on a new career path, consider doing the following for a lifestyle track. Use the talents and skills you recorded in the early chapters of this book as search terms in college course offerings, travel sites, webinars, online courses, alumni continuing education, or community center/park district offerings. You may find a new way to pursue a role or hobby of your choice.

"If you don't love what you do, you won't do it with much conviction or passion."
– Mia Hamm

Dream Job/Hobby

For the dream job exercise, use the information you gathered from the earlier exercises in this chapter to summarize a perfect job for you.

This exercise offers a rare opportunity to do the reverse of a typical job hunt. Instead of searching for a job opportunity/description, you create the ideal one for your career goals.

The point of this exercise is to create a rubric to compare jobs you may apply to while job hunting with what your ideal job would look like. Hopefully, this will save time and get rid of the pain of applying to jobs that are nowhere near a role that would actually make you happy, keep you fulfilled, or match your individual strengths, skills, and abilities.

"Big dreams create the magic that stir
men's souls to greatness."
– Bill McCartney

After you have completed this exercise, review it every time you are looking for a job and before going to any networking events. For the networking events, it will remind you of what you are looking for so that if a new contact happens to mention they are looking to hire someone for a similar job, you will have the ability to focus on strengthening that connection and follow through before someone else gets your dream job. You should always be networking with a purpose.

Create your perfect job/life/lifestyle/volunteer role/hobby:

1. Imagine you are working at your ideal dream job. Where do you see yourself? Where do you want to be? Dream Big!

2. Where is a stretch position that is very attractive to you? It may be in the same industry or corporation. It may be in a new area you want to learn more about.

3. Work/Hobby environment: Describe the job setting you want, focusing on what is most important to you.

4. What makes this opportunity attractive to you? What financial gains, perks, benefits, responsibilities, time, recognition, future opportunities, and logical next steps will this position allow you to pursue?

"Do not wait; the time will never be 'just right.' Start where you stand, and work with whatever tools you may have at your command, and better tools will be found as you go along." – George Herbert.

Chapter 6 Find Your Place: Seek Where You Are Needed in the World

Where you are most needed in the world?

Seek where you can make a difference in the world. To find where you are truly needed requires the hard work of researching before taking steps or deciding.

Research in this circumstance means seeking jobs, careers, activities, and opportunities that need someone with your unique strengths, skills, and experiences. Successful research can be done in several ways. The strategies below end with the same result of gaining information and finding individuals that can help you meet your career goals. Choose the methods that most resonate or seem to fit your style of research best.

Target Marketing Basics

The most important step of doing this research is to connect with individuals in the industry, position, or company that can offer you information, a job, or a referral. These individuals or career helpers can help move your career forward and getting you closer to fulfilling work. Career helpers are the individuals you should focus on and target during your networking and research. To find the most valuable connections, try using a marketing strategy called target marketing.

"Target Marketing means you are putting your customer and their needs at the center of your focus and attention. You are making your customer the most important aspect of doing business, so your products/ services are the best they can be. " – Heather H. Bennett from the blog *Small Business, Big Brand*, "Target Marketing 101"

Target marketing normally refers to finding a customer to purchase a product or service. However, you can employ the same strategies to find the ideal contact for your next career move.

In a career search, the customer is your future employer or someone with knowledge about your ideal job. The needs of the customer are to find an employee with your unique skills, experience, and talents. By targeting future employers or industry experts that are looking for someone like you, you are best able to prepare for that first of many conversations that will lead to your new, more fulfilling work and life.

Given that marketing is becoming more personalized and job hunting more complicated and competitive, the key to success in a career search is to reach the high value target market with the right message. In this case, your target market is someone that can offer you a position, recommend you for an interview, or show you how to become a more attractive candidate for a specific job.

Chapter 6 Exercises

Target Marketing for Career Seekers
Basic techniques to find your high value career helpers.

A target market in this situation is someone who needs to hire, collaborate with or knows the right person to connect you with that will hire you. An ideal target market during a job hunt is someone needing or looking for a professional with your skillset and abilities.

The goal of marketing is to reach the ideal person with the right message at the right time. In this case, the message is that you are the ideal candidate to help them with their business goals.

So how do you find your career search high value target market?

Use these basic techniques to get closer to your target market. Give the ideal employer the opportunity to be helped by you with what they need and grow your career at the same time.

List the qualities of your ideal employer:

Who have been your best-fit employers in the past?

What problem do your unique abilities solve and who needs your abilities the most?

Where can you find employers that use people like you? List locations offline/online, geographic areas, industries, companies and organizations.

Why do past employers love your skills and abilities? Who else have you worked with that has a similar resume?

Who else could become part of your target market that isn't already?

Think beyond basic descriptions of size, location, and industry to include mission, vision, and values statements as well as workload, project type, and clients or customers.

Target Market Communication Plan

Once you have determined your target market, the next step is to create a target market communication plan. Successful marketing means creating communications that share the desired message in the best format through the ideal channels to reach your intended audience.

To successfully communicate you need to know what to say, where to say it, and the right time to reach a person that can help you get your next job.

What forms of social media and traditional communication do they enjoy and use regularly? (Notice where the company or specific individuals engage online or in person at events. Who they follow or industry periodicals they are likely to read? What organizations do they belong to or believe in?)

What advertising and news are they motivated by: types of content, message type, form of media? (Create content in the form of a blog post, journal article or social media post that is similar to what they are most likely to read and react to in a positive way.)

What is the cost in time and money to reach your target market? (Consider the amount of travel, time, and expense to attend a conference or webinar, join an organization, or meet for coffee or lunch. Geographic or other restrictions may limit who and how often you can reach your target market directly. Get creative with virtual coffees or even phone calls to connect with your target market.)

What resources or training do you need to reach your target market?

Which resources or training are in your personal brand marketing budget and are likely to succeed?

When is your target market most likely to be open to communicate with you or any candidate for a role in their organization or to talk to you about your next steps in their industry?

Use a small sample to test your communication in multiple forms of media and with multiple messages. Practice on a friend in that industry or one similar. Choose the messages and times that work the best.

Target Market Listening Plan

As you work on communicating with your target market, use comments, social feeds, social media listening, and trusted colleagues to hear what your target market thinks of your personal brand and message.

Adjust how you are communicating and what your messages say as needed to stay relevant and ahead of what your target market needs. Anticipate what will make them value your abilities, experience, and resume even more. These techniques will help you find your career target market. Reach them with information they are looking for to make the decision to help you meet your career goals.

Start by analyzing the current industry or field that you are in and then move to industries in which you are considering pursuing a career. The further away the future industry is from your current industry will mean more research on your part and more creativity as you may not have access to the network of experts, industry resources, or software needed to analyze that type of work. Be patient. And ask for help.

Use the connections in your network to gain access to information you may not be able to find yourself. Most of the people you meet during this process will have at one time or another been in your shoes looking for a new job or role. Connections are normally more than happy to help another on their career path.

Opportunity Lists by Industry

"If you have a sense of your place in the world, that's the best preparation for anything." – Casey Wilson

What industries have opportunities for you? If you can fill an unmet need for which people are willing to pay, there is a job for you. Be open to possibilities.

Career Track

Create a list of organizations that have or could have the perfect job/position for you. Again, start with your current industry and then spread out to other possibilities.

Lifestyle track

List communities that center around your ideal hobby/lifestyle.

These could be online or in-person communities with actual buildings or people loosely bound together by a common interest. Companies that produce the equipment or locations for the hobby may act as a moderator or central location for the group so start with your favorite tools, equipment, or places.

List as many organizations, conventions, events, or companies that you can with ties to the hobby or lifestyle.

Job Post for Career Track

"Work gives you meaning, and purpose
and life is empty without it."
– Stephen Hawking

After creating a list of organizations, visit their websites or job boards that list open opportunities. Combine these to get an idea of what a perfect job would be for you.

Most listed open jobs are snapped up rapidly, so the action of creating a job post that does not exist is not a wasted effort. Instead it will help you further understand which company, which location, which job title and responsibilities you would love to do.

Write up a job posting you would rush to interview for based on the above notes. Career consultants, coaches, and headhunters use this technique to help them search for jobs with a higher chance that you will accept the position. Create the job offer you couldn't refuse.

> Looking for a candidate for the position of _____
> (job title) at _____ (company).
>
> The position will be located at _____
> (workplace location).
>
> Position responsibilities include:
>
> Benefits include:
>
> Candidate must have these educational requirements:

These skills:

This experience:

"All our dreams come true, if we have the courage to pursue them." – Walt Disney

Sales Pitch for Lifestyle track

Consider how your ideal hobby could become a part-time job or side hustle.

Small (and large) businesses often start out as hobbies.

The cookies that became a household name were once made one dozen at a time in someone's home. An award-winning video game once existed in a stripped-down form on someone's home computer. The keynote speaker at a large sales conference was once a salesperson visiting customers' homes to make the sale one at a time. The top selling fashion brands started out as samples made during the weekends and late at night after a full workday.

Create the ultimate sales pitch. Imagine you are in front of a room full of venture capitalists. Investors with money that are looking for the ideal small business to launch into reality are sitting right in front of you. Imagine, these investors are lined up just waiting to hear about how your hobby could be turned into a successful and thriving business.

What would you do or say that would make your product or service stand out?

What would they look for in what you say about your business to believe that you have what it takes?

What are the areas you would never compromise on if they wanted to invest?

What would you make them promise they wouldn't change if you sold them your side business?

How many sales or what size profit margin would you need to know that this is more than a hobby?

Interviewing an Expert

"When you seek advice, do not withhold facts from the person whose advice you seek." – Abu Baker

Interview at least two people who are currently employed or are an expert in each of your dream jobs/hobbies.

Do not be afraid to call someone you have not met or been introduced to. It is okay to do cold calls if you are brief, polite and completely honest about why you are calling or emailing to respect their time. Be realistic about how much time you need from them, for most people this will take no more than 15 minutes. However, be prepared in case they want to talk longer. Most people love to talk about themselves!

IMPORTANT: Send an email or note to thank them for their time afterward.

Person being interviewed:

Contact phone number and email:

Current title position:

Company/business type:

How do you know them or who gave you their contact information?

Why did you choose your job/hobby?

How did you get here? Experience, education, networking, innovative thinking, opportunity, personal relationship, or connection.

What do you love most about the job/hobby?

What do you wish was better or different?

Finally, what advice would you give to someone considering this type of position?

> *"Seek out a personal coach or mentor in the workplace. He/she should push you when you need it by encouraging and motivating you. Don't be afraid of their honesty." – Cathy Engelbert*

Researching Company or Community Analysis

One of my favorite classes during my MBA studies was Finance. The research and analysis required for the due diligence to understand if a company was going to be successful, fascinated me then and now.

With the fluctuations of the stock market based not only on sales and profit data but also on a myriad of perceptions and industry influences, figuring out the likelihood of success is similar to solving a complex mystery.

The research techniques and analysis methods used to buy or sell a stock can also be used to help you find the ideal job. The questions below are a simplified version of a complete due diligence study and a great place to start researching your potential future employer.

For each company or community, fill out as many of the following sections as possible. Ask questions of human resources, former or current employees, or research online in social media sites and industry publications. Use a spreadsheet or table to keep the information organized.

Note: These questions are also useful during a job interview or in conversation with a potential employer to help you get to know the company, demonstrate a high level of interest in the company, and allow you to focus on more in depth questions to ask your interviewer that will make you stand out from other candidates.

A. Who are their customers? What is their relationship with customers?

B. What products or services do they offer?

C. Who are their competitors?

D. SWOT analysis: What are their Strengths, Weaknesses, Opportunities, and Threats?

E. What unique niche does the company fill in their field?

F. Where are they located?

G. What is their social media presence? (platforms, online chatter, positive or negative)

H. What is the culture like? (talk to an HR person or current/former employee)

I. What is their Mission (Vision) Statement? (what does the company do and stand for?)

J. What is their financial situation? (any red flags or concerns)

K. What positions within the company are they looking to fill? Look at all open positions as this may indicate an area that they are growing or having difficulty finding good candidates.

L. What is the contact information for Human Resources and hiring team?

Lifestyle Track

Where can you find a community of people with similar interests to yours?

Examine and research organizations, foundations, events and clubs that celebrate and are centered around your favorite hobby. Attend conventions, conferences, masterminds and online webinars for that industry

Ask the questions above in the career track about each club or organization to learn which may be worth getting to know better. Pay attention to dues or membership requirement as these can become barriers to entry or make one organization a better fit for you versus another.

Part Three: Communicating and Maintaining Your Personal Brand

For Chapter 7, we will map out a strategic plan to help you share and communicate your personal brand. Prepare to create an actual action list with time frames and goals. By the end of Chapter 7, you will have created a prioritized list of action items that will guide you and prepare you step by step for your greatest opportunities for fulfillment.

> _"What I know is, is that if you do work that you love, and the work fulfills you, the rest will come." – Oprah Winfrey_

Finally, in Chapter 8, I have included templates and recommendations for updating and maintaining your personal brand.

Your personal brand deserves the continuous care needed to keep it working hard for you and more importantly keep it authentic to who you are at each moment. Humans are wonderful, fascinating beings that have the gift of being able to learn, change, and grow throughout our lives. Your personal brand will grow and change with you and will need finetuning from time to time as you and your life change.

By regularly maintaining and checking on how your personal brand fits with your current personal and professional needs, you will be ready for the next opportunity that comes your way.

Chapter 7 Creating Your Strategic Personal Brand Plan: Specific Tasks and Actions to Achieve Your Ideal Work and Life

*"You are never too old to set another goal
or to dream a new dream." – C.S. Lewis*

Throughout this process, you have taken the time to get to know yourself, find your inspiration, find your place in this world and, finally, turn your dreams into reality. Both working on discovering your true nature and seeking your authentic self are not easy or simple tasks. You should be proud of the mental effort, time spent, and work done to help find a fulfilling career.

Discovering your passion, purpose, inspiration, and motivation is vital to your happiness and success. Realize that every exercise you do and every question you answer help you move one step closer to a life that you are excited to wake up to everyday and experience. Every insight allows you to better understand your needs for fulfillment and where you can make an impact in the world.

*"Keep your dreams alive. Understand to
achieve anything requires faith and belief
in yourself, vision, hard work,
determination, and dedication. Remember
all things are possible for those who
believe." – Gail Devers*

In creating your strategic personal brand plan, remember to be patient. The time you invest in this pursuit will pay off in more than just success in your field, it will also pay off in your life. As part of modern society, we all experience the overwhelming lack of time in our lives. However, reprioritizing your goals and responsibilities will improve your life overall. Make one of your goals to regain control over your time. To gain control over time, you need to create efficient habits for your everyday tasks, develop clear objectives for your career, and most importantly, keep your personal brand authentic.

Ashley Williams, author of *Time for Happiness, Why the Pursuit of Money isn't Bringing You Joy and What Will*, explains that "Time poverty exists across all economic strata, and its effects are profound. Research shows that those who feel time-poor experience lower levels of happiness and higher levels of anxiety, depression, and stress. They experience less joy. They laugh less. They exercise less and are less healthy.
Their productivity at work is diminished. They are more likely to get divorced. And in our analysis of the Gallup survey data, my team and I even found that time stress had a stronger negative effect on happiness than being unemployed did."

As a strong proponent of preventive healthcare and decreasing stress to increase productivity and fulfillment in life, I am a dedicated student of time management. Refer to my time management discussion in Chapter 4 to highlight my studies on time management and the top recommendations I have gleaned from years of studying productivity. As mentioned earlier, I consider myself a lifelong student in the studies of productivity and time management – not an expert but a dedicated enthusiast. The clock will march on, only twenty-four hours exist in everyday, but with an organized and strategic plan those hours can accomplish much more.

Part of a good productivity plan includes scheduling time to decompress. Options abound for how to decompress including flipping mindlessly through a magazine, playing games, or wandering aimlessly without a definite time or distance goal.

One of my favorite forms of downtime is simply sitting and looking at the water in a lake or ocean, especially at sunset or sunrise. In the book *Blue Mind: The Surprising Science That Shows How Being Near, In, On or Under Water Can Make You Happier, Healthier, More Connected and Better at Why You Do* by author, Wallace J. Nichols, Nichols states "Being on, in, and near water can be among the most cost-effective ways of reducing stress and anxiety." This explains the popularity of beach and lake vacations as well as how humans are drawn to the sea.

Schedule in time for yourself to reduce stress and allow for the natural brain waves of creativity to take over. You may just find an answer to a tough question or the solution to a difficult problem. Or, at the very least, give yourself the chance to take a few deep breaths, clear your mind, and start over.

Failure as a Requirement

There are times when you need to move forward and make a conscience choice, even when that choice will lead to a high probability of failure.

My advice to you…go ahead, fail.

It might seem strange to encourage failure. However, in a study by a Northwestern University team led by Yang Wang, Benjamin F. Jones, and Dashun Wang titled, *Early-Career Setback and Future Career Impact*, the "failure" group outperformed the "success" group in producing highly regarded scientific papers by a factor of about 21%. The theory behind the research suggests that the early "failure" to secure funding from grants as opposed to definitely securing funding encouraged the scientist in the data set to work harder and achieve success at a greater rate. Basically, "early failure should not be taken as a negative signal—but rather the opposite."

There is a purpose and a point in failure, if you consider most of the greatest advances in technology have occurred after multiple attempts ended in failure. In fact, failure is an important aspect of both innovation and success. Scientific experimentation often follows a winding disjointed path where failures lead to unexpected solutions to problems.

> *"But failure has to be an option in art and in exploration--because it's a leap of faith. And no important endeavor that required innovation was done without risk. You have to be willing to take those risks."*
> *– James Cameron*

163

When considering a choice of action for your personal brand or career, keep in mind that you are a work in progress. It is okay to fail the first few times as you try to get closer to creating and sharing your personal brand. Just keep trying. A strong sense of hope and a tolerance for failure will serve you well if you already accept it as part of the process.

In the act of reinventing and redefining yourself at a point of transformation due to a change in career, lifestyle or life stage offers a unique chance to turn past failures into an advantage. The advantage is that you have one less option to try and consider. There is even more clarification as to what is authentic and true for your personal brand. Avenues and paths not previously open to you may now be open since you have proven yourself capable of trying and resilient enough to get up and try again.

> *"Don't be too hard on yourself. There are*
> *plenty of people willing to do that for you."*
> *– Susan Gale.*

Learning what does not work can show exactly what will work. And without learning from our mistakes we are destined to repeat them.

The benefits of failures extend into your career as well. To paraphrase an AJR song, "100 bad stories" make you more interesting and colorful at parties, during interviews, online, or at the next networking event. Dare to be memorable. Dare to be your unique self. Stand out from the crowd.

"A hundred bad days made
a hundred good stories
A hundred good stories make me
interesting at parties
Yeah, no, I ain't scared of you
No, I ain't scared of you no more"
– AJR

I interpret the words of AJR in the last two stanzas to mean that he wasn't scared of failure anymore. If he isn't scared of bad days or failures, then why should we be?

Be prepared for interviews, the next time a recruiter asks you directly, "Tell me about a time you failed." own the question. Share the life lessons, strategies, and new directions that the experience helped you discover. Let the lessons of failure guide you to the next ideal job or position. Remind the interviewer that without failure the ideal candidate would not be available for that next opening.

"I've failed over and over and over again
in my life and that is why I succeed."
– Michael Jordan

Go fail already. Or if you already have, know that it is okay. Take notes, share, process, and move on to the next opportunity, the next risk that will eventually lead you to success.

Success Merging

Lately, I have been thinking a lot about exactly what events and circumstances need to occur for a person to find success. Inspired by books I have read, a few conversations, and podcast episodes about success, I have decided to form a loose theory about what elements are required for success. I call this convergence of events "Success Merging".

Similar to a driver merging onto a highway there are two aspects of the merge to make it successful. First, you control when you enter the highway. You have control over how fast and when and where your vehicle moves. The second part – which you have absolutely no control over -- is the other vehicles already on the highway. A successful merge requires a combination of things you can control and things you cannot control.

The first way to look at this merge point is to describe it as the point where hustle meets luck.

Think about the stories of Hollywood stars that got the leading roles in blockbuster hits. The backstory often involves the luck of a famous producer hiring them as a valet or other lower level job and then suddenly being inspired or out of desperation hiring them for a much greater role or position. A glamourous Hollywood dream story that – no big surprise here – would make a great movie.

But wait… the other part of the backstory that often gets downplayed or ignored is the long hours and years the aspiring actor spent going to audition after audition. The numerous talent agents they approached and who rejected them. The piles of scripts and pitches that were tossed or told they were not worth reading. The hustle of taking on whatever job the hopeful struggling artist could do just to stay alive in Southern California or New York. The point of success occurred when the years of hustle met the moment of luck.

"When your greatest talent intersects with your greatest passion, you have discovered your sweet spot in life." James D. Denney and Pat Williams from *The Success Intersection: What Happens When Your Talent Meets Your Passion.*

Another way to look at Success Merging is where hard work meets opportunity.

Consider the rags to riches stories of the restaurant mogul that started by buying a broken-down building and spending every waking hour and cent cleaning, repairing, and refurbishing it just to barely pass the health inspection and open, spending the very last dime she has on paper menus with coupons to flood the neighborhood. She spends every hour the restaurant is open in front on the sidewalk talking up potential customers and handing out menus.

Ready to give up only a week after a sadly quiet opening, the owner notices a couple standing outside deciding whether to dine there or move on. The restaurant owner walks out to them and in a passionate and colorful speech describes the special of the day with such love, fervor and energy, the couple looks at each other and shrugs, "Why not?"

After what arguably is one of the best meals of their lives, they go off and tell their friends and coworkers about this great new eatery they discovered. One of these friends happens to be the husband of a restaurant critic. The critic decides to take a chance and tries the restaurant. Again, a delicious meal turns into a glowing review that is the opportunity in the success merge point that propels the restaurant owner to her first of many successful restaurant openings.

A third way to look at Success Merging is where persistence meets happy accident or chance.

A researcher spending years working in a lab conducting innumerable experiments, trying every variable possible until a strange accident causes a cure or a reaction that was never hypothesized or predicted. Imagine the impossibilities that could one day occur. The eye drops intended to cure a disease that make cataracts surgery unnecessary. The heart drug that improves lung function. The psoriasis cream that cures skin cancer without surgery.

Hundreds of thousands of tests took place in labs, hospitals all funded by grants, corporations, or government programs only to discover something completely unexpected and yet helpful, useful, and even monetizable. The Success Merging of persistence and happy accident.

One final example of Success Merging is where fate meets preparedness. The process of day in and day out practicing and preparing for that one event or moment of genius, brilliant, perfection.

"With a serendipity mindset, every interaction might open a new path — for finding love, meeting an investor, making a friend, forging a new interest, or landing a new job." – Christian Busch, Author of *The Serendipity Mindset*

Consider the years of practice and dedication required to propel an Olympic athlete to the podium and the alignment of fate that must occur to be, at that specific competition on that exact day, the best.

To not have a bad day or a distracted moment or be sick or pick up the wrong equipment. Think of the swimmer that managed without a pair of functional goggles to swim a gold medal earning performance.

The millions of angles and precious alignment of time to get a soccer ball from the corner kick, through the traffic of players on both sides, and through to that single player with the perfectly timed header to angle the ball to the one corner of the goal the keeper can't reach. The second part of that goal is the fate of the defenders and players to not happen to move at the wrong moment to block the goal entirely.

> *"There is no substitute for persistence.*
> *The person who makes persistence his*
> *watch-word, discovers that 'Old Man*
> *Failure' finally becomes tired, and makes*
> *his departure. Failure cannot cope with*
> *persistence." – Napoleon Hill.*

What do all of these have in common? How can we learn from these examples of Success Merging? The common thread is a choice by the individual to actively choose to make their lives open to success. The individual must choose to do the active first part of the equation: hustle, hard work, persistence, preparedness, practice – repeatedly. Then they must have the hope and watchfulness that by being ready for fate, chance, opportunity and luck, their success will occur.

In our lives, what can we do to be prepared? The fact that you have chosen to read this book shows that you are already in the right frame of mind.

What else can you do?

The following is a list of ways to prepare for success. Consider them inspiration to push you closer to success. Try to choose a new one to add each week, month or year, increasing your odds of reaching the moment of success.

Success Starters

- Networking

- Learn a new skill

- Practice

- Delayed gratification

- Sacrifice

- Focus on the goal

- Use creativity to spark innovation

- Stretch to meet new challenges

- Try something new

- Do something that scares you

- Share and celebrate small successes

- Follow your passion

- Let your passion fuel your daily work

- Forgive yourself

- Dust off and get up…again and again

- Take failure as a sign to try something again or something different

- Don't stay down long, learn to get up and move on.

> *"Success is liking yourself, liking what you do, and liking how you do it."*
> *– Maya Angelou*

Find something you are so passionate about and love doing that even if it is hard or there are obstacles, you can't help but do it. Find your calling. Be passionate, let the fire within keep you going even when the goal seems far off or the obstacles insurmountable.

Use the section in Chapter 2 about what to do if you are stuck to help you move beyond a setback, over a hurdle, or past an obstacle. We are all human. We will fail. We will be knocked down. Only by deciding to act can we get up, learn from our mistakes and failures, try new and creative solutions, and ultimately reach success.

Perseverance in the Face of Disinterest

Working hard to achieve a personal goal can be lonely and is often difficult. Deciding to push yourself beyond your comfort level does not necessarily mean your usual support team will be there to back you up, especially if you are making major life changes that will affect their lives as well.

This frustrating result of change is part of the process and not to be looked on as an inconvenience or obstacle, but more as an inevitable and defining event.

My viewpoint after years of experience with other human beings is that most of the time people will do less than you expect of them.

Why?

1. They can't read your mind.

2. They have their own needs, wants, and goals.

3. They are honestly not aware of you or your goals.

Jaded? Oh yeah. Slightly depressing? Yes. Defensive? Definitely. Realistic? Well, mostly. Even with these less than happy views, I encourage you to be optimistic and have hope. There is a mindset change that can help with this daunting problem.

"You learn in life that the only person you can really correct, and change is yourself." – Katharine Hepburn

Accepting that you can't actually change others is not a failing or even giving up, but more realizing the parameters you are working within. Consider changing others as a boundary you can't pass through but can influence by your actions and reactions. The benefit of this mindset is that if they choose to change themselves or simply reach out a helping hand, their mere actions become a pleasant and unexpected benefit to your goals. Call it serendipity.

Don't be discouraged by people you thought you could count on falling short of helping you. Too many times I have seen people in my life or others' lives come up short when they could have – if they chose – made a situation better for someone else -- selflessly -- but they don't.

Recently a classmate from college was about to have a major life event. She was getting married to the love of her life. Planning a wedding is a lot of work. A project that could use some help. She reached out to her network of colleagues in the events industry that she had carefully developed and graciously contributed to for close to fifteen years, only to be shunned or ghosted by almost all of them. Why? Maybe their excuse was selfishness, too much work, or indifference. Maybe they did not have the authority to make decisions. Maybe she wasn't as close to them as she thought. Maybe they had strict work rules that required them to never offer favors for weddings. Who knows?

What I do know is that, given the opportunity, they chose to not help another person willingly.

You can only change yourself.

Why bother trying to convert others to help with a situation? Well, there is one caveat. You should keep asking for help. Keep trying because there is always the hope that just this once they might help. But don't beat yourself up if they don't. Forgive and forget. There is always hope they might make a different choice next time and become an example for others.

"When things are a disappointment, try not to be so discouraged." – Carol Burnett

In the meantime, either get used to disappointment or expect nothing and hope for everything... a pleasant delight. We get to choose how we view the world. Choose carefully and consciously how you view the world.

Be patient. Hang in there. Draw from your own strength and belief in yourself to power through until someone is willing to take a risk and help you out. In the meantime, look for small opportunities to spread a little kindness.

"Compassion for others begins with kindness to ourselves." – Pema Chondron

Communication Skills for Interviews and More
Part of preparing for your new job, industry, or start-up is improving your communication skills. Communication for anyone in a career transition involves not only interviews, but presentations and public speaking. Practicing the skills

needed for great interviews, effective presentations, and persuasive speeches is vital to career success.

When you start at a new role, it is expected that you will bring something to the team or business. Being able to sell your viewpoint through effective communication is vital to establishing yourself as an important contributor.

Being able to effectively communicate helps you establish yourself as a key thought or opinion leader. As your career advances and you become an expert in your industry or field, becoming a key opinion leader can add to your reputation and bottom line.

Consider the advantages of being invited to co-author a book or chapter, being asked to give keynote speeches at your industry's annual conventions, or being asked to join the C-Suite as the Chief Officer for your role. Dream big about how improving all aspects of your abilities and skills can open more opportunities.

Public Speaking is listed as one of the greatest human fears. It's right up there with death, loneliness, and spiders. Clearly, this is an opportunity for growth and development for most people. Take action to become a better public speaker.

Read books or take courses, join a toastmasters or local speaking community. The National Speakers Association (NSA) is an association for professional speakers. Many of the NSA state chapters offer courses, webinars, and lectures on how to become a better speaker and open these academies to the public.

Another excellent opportunity to improve your skills as a public speaker is to offer to chair a committee, moderate a panel discussion, take a class in improvisation or acting, or participate in a poetry slam or open mic night.

Focusing on these basic tips for great public speaking will help you feel more confident before you start.

- First, take a deep breath and wait a moment or pause before beginning.

- Talk to the audience and their needs, not your own.

- Remember to thank everyone involved in the event, but don't take too long.

- Pretend to be confident and having fun. Looking the part of a calm presenter will help you feel more relaxed.

- Practice, practice, practice – in front of a mirror or video record yourself speaking to get a better idea of your physical movements or times when your voice is difficult to understand.

- Smile and breath.

Public speaking is one of those inevitable situations almost everyone finds themselves in. Improve your skills as a public speaker to benefit your career and audience by trying one tip or recommendation at a time.

Social Media Simplified

Who has time to keep up with all the new advances, topics, platforms and uses of social media? Unless you are a social media expert by trade, you are not likely to want or need to be great at all forms of social media. It is better to rely on the experts for business goals and have team members that truly are experts to help with each platform.

Brigid Schulte in the book, *Overwhelmed*, describes attending a Time studies conference. During the conference, the presenters and attendees discussed why our lives seem to be spinning out of control. "Technology spins that overwhelm faster. At the conference, researchers sought to unravel how the explosive speed and sheer quantity of information, and the rapid and mystifying shifts in the economy and politics, and the uncertainty about the future, are swamping every."

Given that technology and social media seem to be at the heart of that lack of control, it seems a logical place to make changes for the better within our lives. By learning more about social media, we can better understand how it affects our lives and ways to alter it so that it makes our lives better and simpler. Social media is a tool to help us communicate. If we take the time to learn how to use it, social media can be an effective and useful tool in the pursuit of fun and fulfilling careers.

The "social media pyramid" groups the various forms of social media by the depth with which topics are discussed in each platform. The importance of the pyramid is to show where you will create a higher level of engagement, return on investment, and greater number of sales. For example, watching a YouTube video about lawn mowers is not as likely to sell more lawn mowers than a spirited discussion of the benefits of one brand versus another on a forum (virtual community) of riding lawnmower enthusiasts.

In the social media pyramid, the higher the listed platform is in the diagram, the less likely the discussions will be deep and involve a high level of engagement on an industry specific topic. Arguably some of the groups formed on Facebook and LinkedIn will actually reside closer to the bottom of the pyramid as they represent more in-depth conversations for an industry or topic. However, these platforms as a whole, based on how the algorithms decide who sees each post, tend to have shallow, quick discussions.

For the purpose of this book and personal branding, it is important to develop social proof by being on multiple social media platforms. Which platforms you choose will depend on what your individual goals are for your career, work, and life. My minimum recommendations for small business owners are to have a presence on Facebook, Instagram, and LinkedIn to support a business website. My minimum recommendations for job seekers are to have a presence on LinkedIn and at least two of the following, Twitter, Facebook, Instagram and/or a website depending on industry type.

Later, once your business or personal brand is more established, adding blogs, newsletters, YouTube channels, or a Pinterest account will round out your social media presence and help establish you as a respected member of your field or industry.

Social Media Pyramid

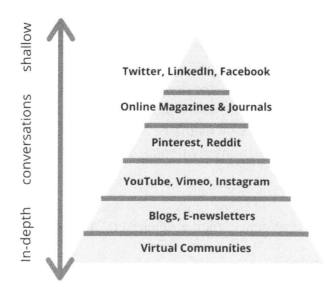

The Social Media Pyramid lists the most commonly used forms of social media in a format that describes the depth of discussions on specific topics.

The top of the pyramid represents broad reach in numbers of audience and the lowest part ot the pyramid represents fewer but more targeted audience members.

The higher the platform is listed in the pyramid, the more shallow the discussions will be for a specific topic. With the most in-depth discussions occurring near the bottom of the pyramid.

This version created by Heather H. Bennett

The best advice I give to clients about social media is to only invest time and money in the social media platforms that (1) resonate with you, (2) are directly tied to communicating your message to your target markets, and (3) communicate that message in the most effective way. Otherwise, you are wasting your time.

Social Media Recommendations

Facebook

Description:

> "Facebook is a website which allows users, who sign-up for free profiles, to connect with friends, work colleagues or people they don't know, online. It allows users to share pictures, music, videos, and articles, as well as their own thoughts and opinions with however many people they like." – webwise.ie

Best used for:

> Cost effective, highly efficient online advertising

Best practices:

- Create a Facebook page that shows you as a professional

- Post on it to support your blog

- Keep it updated

- Link to your website

- Use consistent photos and images

- Feature and share other related articles online

- Actively schedule time to comment on industry/topic sites

Twitter
Description:

> "Twitter is a social media site, and its primary purpose is to connect people and allow people to share their thoughts with a big audience. Twitter allows users to discover stories regarding today's biggest news and events, follow people or companies that post content they enjoy consuming, or simply communicate with friends. Additionally, PR teams and marketers can use Twitter to increase brand awareness and delight their audience." – Caroline Forsey

Best used for:

> Growing an audience or followers, communicating with your tribe, consumers, or fans, sharing, and finding information quickly, keeping up with industry information, generating traffic to your website.

Best practices:

- Use a scheduler (Hootsuite, Buffer)

- Create tweets to support blog

- Include a photo or visual with every Twitter post

- Include a CTA (Call to Action)

- Use Bit.ly etc. to shorten the URL of Blog posts

- Use Twitter analytics for best posts

- Consider running a 2-week A/B split test to determine best times to post and highest rated content

Instagram

Description:

> "Instagram is a video and photo-sharing social network. It launched in 2010 as a mobile device app and was acquired by Facebook two years later." – Maggie Tillman and Elyse Betters

Best used for:

> Getting to know your audience and communicating with them instantly. A picture is worth a thousand words. Use Instagram for sharing your images. Engagement is a great use for Instagram.

Best practices:

- Use 10-15 hashtags per post

- Keep a consistent look of 2-4 layouts that will form a pleasing checkboard when viewed as a whole

- Best for images that include people's faces

- Link to website or sign up or blog post

- Keep background colors, fonts consistent

- Follow back

- Post 1-3 times per week

Pinterest

Description:

>   Pinterest is an image focused platform with only short captions for words. Keywords are incredibly important.

Best used for:

>   Curating a collection of images from other people, companies, and websites. Often used to search for ideas for an event, or design/fashion decisions.

Best practices:

- Focus on the best keyword to include

- Best for images that do not include human faces

- Keep a consistent look of 2-4 layouts that will form a pleasing checkboard when viewed as a whole

- Use only high-quality images

- Link to website or sign up or blog post

- Keep background colors, fonts consistent

- "Follow" back

- Post 1 time a week

LinkedIn
Description:

> "LinkedIn is a social network that focuses on professional networking and career development." – Dave Johnson

Best used for:

> B2B (Business to business) sharing of business and industry related topics and discussions. Sharing job experience and acting as a live resume.
> Establishing thought leadership and social proof of professional knowledge.

Best practices:

- Create a solid LinkedIn page for your audience, not you! Design your page and your posts to fill their needs as they seek information on you

- Post on it to support your blog

- Keep it updated

- Ask for endorsements and recommendations from clients, coworkers, current and past

- Link to your website

- Fill all 50 skill lists, change the top 3 based on the needs of your business so you rank higher

- Use consistent photos and images

- Feature and share other related articles online as well as short video clips

- All information should support the headline

- Keep information focused on core business, do not add tangential information/businesses unless they are relevant to your primary business goals

- Comment and engage with colleagues so you are seen as an expert in your field and a helpful contributor.

"The party is in the comments"
– Troy Sandidge

Blogs
Description:

"A blog (shortening of "weblog") is an online journal or informational website displaying information in the reverse chronological order, with the latest posts appearing first. It is a platform where a writer or even a group of writers share their views on an individual subject." -Anya Skrba

Best used for:

Driving traffic to your website to sell your products or services.

Best practices:

- Focus your blog on the needs of a single audience

185

- Use descriptive keywords for every blog

- Include a great image that will represent and grab attention

- Make sure you include a meta description

- Check your keywords for popularity and likelihood to be found during a search

- Blog length depends on your purpose: longer blogs tend to be highly packed with data and information, shorter blogs may rely more heavily on simple messages

- Include a CTA (call to action) to drive traffic to your website or LinkedIn profile

- Correct image size to work for your blog site recommendations

- Link to your own site as well as other websites to improve your search engine optimization (SEO)

- Use a URL shortener to make it easier to share

Website
Description:

> A website is "a location connected to the Internet that maintains one or more pages on the World Wide Web." – Dictionary.com

Best used for:

> Sharing information, selling products, or encouraging the visitor to your website to connect with you. Most importantly, it is used to help a visitor solve a problem.

Best practices:

- Clean and professional looking, easy to scroll through

- Add all your social links on your webpage (Facebook, Instagram, Twitter, Instagram, Pinterest)

- Update the photos of you, your business, products and services

- Use video when possible

- Clean, easy to read design

- Regularly check links, keep current, add new information

- Keep home page interesting by featuring one pinned blog a month

Email Newsletters
Description:

> "Email newsletters are an email communication sent out to inform your audience of the latest news, tips,

or updates about your product or company." –
campaignmonitor.com

Best used for:

Keeping you and your personal brand top of mind for your audience, followers, and for consumers to drive them to buy your products and/or services.

Best practices:

- Short and sweet, once per month

- Blog post front and center

- Give a specific CTA (call to action)

    o Follow me on list of social media

    o Buy product, app or eBook

    o Click here to see where I am speaking or attending next

    o Share this newsletter with a friend

- Check Links

- Include event registration page links twice

- Fill with useful information

REMEMBER: The most important takeaway about social media is to only be on the platforms where:

- you enjoy spending time,

- your target markets are found, and

- where you will actually monitor and contribute to consistently.

Chapter 7 Exercises

The exercises in Chapter 7 are designed to create a specific action plan. Your Strategic Personal Brand Plan will consist of actions listed with due dates to keep you on track. By completing each action, you will get closer and closer to reaching your goals.

> *"If you write something down on paper, it becomes an actual goal. Before you write it down, it's a thought, a dream that may or may not get done."*
> *– Summer Sanders*

Plan for Career/Volunteer Work Track

Creating a plan takes time and effort. Sometimes the hardest step after deciding to take action is determining which way to go.   Take the time to write down what you want to accomplish so you can determine the timing of each action, when you will reach each milestone and, more importantly, see which actions may require help or extra research. By writing down each action, you will start to see the steps that will get you closer to your dream job and ideal career.

> *"To achieve great things, we must not only act, but also dream. Not only plan but also believe." – Anatole France*

Remember things change and timing often needs to respond to outside influences. Don't be discouraged if you have to rewrite your plan a few times. A career transition does not happen overnight. Start with one step and one question at a time.

Planning your Lifestyle Track

The series of questions below will help as you make changes in your life or hobby. Just because you are not changing your career or work, does not mean that the rest of your life must remain stagnant. A growth mindset can occur beyond the office or workplace into the space of our private lives. Bringing excitement and success to your personal life is equally important for true work-life balance.

"It is not in the stars to hold our destiny,
but in ourselves." – William Shakespeare

1. Reread your personal brand statement, ideal job description, and advice from experts.

2. What training or skills do you need to do this hobby or live your lifestyle with excellence? What skills do you need to improve or learn? What training or skills do you need to stand out from the competition for what you want? What skills do you need to brush up on or receive training to excel in your lifestyle? Consider apprenticeships, internships, online courses, formal course work, webinars, group learning, and individual training.

3. Who is your "in" to the industry? Who is your inspiration in this lifestyle? Who are the influencers? Do you know someone from college, or even your professional, or social circles that could help you learn more about this hobby or lifestyle? Find at least one person who has been doing this hobby for at least five years to act as a mentor. Consider your business network, convention connections, company sports teams, LinkedIn contacts, other tangential companies that work with the company directly, faith or school communities, social media groups, and your personal network.

4. Update your resume and LinkedIn to reflect your personal brand so you are prepared to share what you want. Create and practice out loud your elevator speech with a trusted friend or colleague to explain what you are seeking in an ideal job or hobby. Consider the elevator speech as a more polished version of what you would say when meeting someone at a party.

5. Keep up to date on industry news through communities, publications, webinars, conventions, conferences, Twitter, LinkedIn, blogs, Reddit, and key word searches.

6. List your action items in chronological order. Specify the dates to have each accomplished. Hold yourself accountable. Make a visual reminder that you check daily or weekly to keep inspired about

your goals. Include reminders in your calendar with notifications or write the tasks in a To Do list. Think about how you are going to fund your new venture or hobby. An activity that stays in budget is a lot more enjoyable.

7. Optimize your performance. What would excellence look like? What makes someone exceptional or an expert? What level of performance would bring you great fulfillment? Sometimes excellence does not equal happiness or fulfillment. For a hobby, focus on excellence only if that will bring you enjoyment while preparing for or doing the hobby.

8. Make necessary course corrections. What changes or updates in your action plan do you need to make to stay on course and keep moving towards the career and life goals you talked about in Chapter 1?

9. Consider whether this is the greatest impact you could have on the world. Where else might your talents have a broader or deeper reach? Does this hobby or lifestyle fulfill at least one of your top goals in life? A hobby does not need to fulfill a life goal or make the world a better place. The important part of a hobby is to bring you enjoyment. If it happens to make the world a better place or fulfill a life goal, that is a bonus.

"Ever since I was a child, I have had this instinctive urge for expansion and growth. To me, the function and duty of a quality human being is the sincere and honest development of one's potential."
– Bruce Lee

Personal Brand Strategy

Fill out the following statements considering everything you have learned about yourself while reading this book. Feel free to flip back and forth through your notes to better understand which of your words to fill in each blank. Act to make your life fulfilling!

"Don't wait until everything is just right. It will never be perfect. There will always be challenges, obstacles, and less than perfect conditions. So what? Get started now. With each step you take, you will grow stronger and stronger, more and more skilled, more and more self-confident, and more and more successful." – Mark Victor Hansen

OPTION 1: Personal Branding taught me the following about myself

I learned I want to spend more time doing:

    1.

    2.

    3.

    because they help me....

    or give me joy through using my unique talents and skills.

In the future, I want to do:

    be:....

    and spend more time doing:....

In 3-5 years, I see myself doing:

    with this organization

    so, I can achieve my goals of: ....

"It is never too late to be what you might have been." – George Eliot

OPTION 2: Elevator Speech

Another way to write your personal brand plan is to create an elevator speech. Use this short less-than-one-minute speech to share the following information at a networking event or conference. The elevator speech should include: your name, what you do for a living in easy to understand terms, what you need help with, how you can help others and finally a direct Call to Action (CTA). The CTA should be specific. List how to contact or connect with you and have time parameters within a month or the next year.

An example from a fictitious person is ...

> "Hi, my name is Natalie. I own and manage a coffee shop in the center of town. I am looking to include a few take home meals to sell to customers on their way home from work or to eat at lunch. Do you know of any caterers looking to expand their business beyond events? As this is still Spring, I am hoping to have the meals ready to sell by the back-to-school, late-August time period, so finding someone in the next month is important. Here is my card. Send me an email if you think of anyone."

Practice this elevator speech before going to any work or networking events or even non-professional events. You never know who you might meet or who they might know.

Accountability for your Personal Brand Strategy

A well-created and authentic personal brand is only powerful with accountability to achieve the desired goals. A To-Do list or project management outline helps with accountability because we can clearly see the steps needed to complete a goal without being overwhelmed. Having a list of actions allows us to cross off each one and therefore focus our attention on one at a time. This leads to a higher likelihood that each task will be accomplished before we become distracted by another task.

Commit to creating doable action items to help you achieve your Personal Brand Strategy. Then, find a way to keep yourself accountable for doing each action by finding an accountability group or buddy.

Tip: After creating this accountability list, keep it in an often-viewed location or copy to your calendar every couple of weeks. Complete the statements below to yourself to stay focused on reaching your goals with your personal brand.

To reach my career and life goals, I need to accomplish the following actions:

In 1 month, I need to: ….

In 6 months, I need to: ….

In 1 year, I need to: ….

I will continue to find time to take care of myself and reevaluate my personal branding statement as I grow and change. I will create a new action plan when what I am doing with my life is not bringing me joy and fulfillment or conflicts with helping me reach my goals.

Chapter 8 Keeping Your Personal Brand Strong: Checkups, Maintenance, and Updates

Congratulations! You have completed the hard work for your personal brand by:

- getting to know yourself and your personal brand authentically,

- writing a core description,

- creating a personal branding statement and/or elevator speech,

- crafting messages and templates to communicate your personal brand, and

- designing an action plan of tasks to reach your personal goals

Consider this chapter a maintenance plan for keeping your personal brand strong.

Complete the exercises as needed.

Put aside time in your calendar for the next year for the maintenance tasks. By scheduling the time, you will keep up with the maintenance and not be overwhelmed by trying to squeeze in time between your other responsibilities.

Personal Brand Maintenance Plan

At the very least, schedule one day a year (early January or for those attuned to the school-based year, August) to review your goals and plans for the year for both your personal and professional life.

It may seem like a luxury or unnecessary but consider how much time you will save over the course of the year. You will save time by clearly understanding which goals you want to achieve, the priority ranking of your goals, and the tasks needed to be completed to achieve them.

You cannot accomplish the goals you don't know, can't name, and haven't written down.

Personal Brand Pivot Points

Keeping your Personal Brand up to date as you evolve and change as a person is important. Certain times are more likely to cause enough change to demand a revision or at least spending time evaluating whether your personal brand is still authentic to you.

Personal Brand Pivot Points are times that will require you to evaluate and adjust your personal brand.

The list below makes recommendations and provides examples of these points. Add any other times that resonate with you personally as points of major change or times for a pivot.

- Graduation from school or course of study
- New job
- Completion of an internship
- Moving to a new city
- Major lifestyle change (marriage or divorce, new roommate, new baby, traumatic event)
- Health or medical event

- Substantial financial gain or loss

- Other life-changing event

Be aware that a few of these points might benefit from working on your personal brand before the event or while planning for it. Consider redoing at least a few of the exercises to update your strategic personal brand plan and notes.

Having a strong, authentic, and time-specific personal brand will give you another tool to ease the transition from your prior situation to a new situation. Give yourself the gift of thinking about your personal brand and preparing it to travel to the new life moment with you successfully.

Networking with a Purpose

I've touched on networking throughout the book but now let's delve into it.

Networking is more than a business buzz word. It is a tool and a skill set needed to move your career forward.

Networking as defined by David J.P. Fisher in *Networking in the 21st Century* "is building a web of relationships with others for mutual support in finding business solutions." This definition is simple, elegant, thorough and to the point. It embodies not only what networking is but also what it can or should accomplish.

Networking is so much easier and, dare I say, fun if you network with a personal brand.

Remember, a strong personal brand is one that is authentic, easily communicated, and helps others understand your goals professionally and/or personally.

Networking is the perfect time to share your personal brand with the end result of either:

meeting someone that can help you achieve your goals, or

discovering opportunities for you to help others achieve their goals.

By knowing and clearly communicating your personal brand, you open up more opportunities to give and receive during networking.

The cornerstone or calling card of successful networking is the elevator speech. This is the short (normally under one minute) speech you developed in chapter 7 that is a clear description of who you are, what you do, what help you are looking for, and, most importantly, how you can help the listener. See Option 2: Elevator Speech in the Chapter 7 exercises for an example and outline.

Having a solid, well-rehearsed, yet natural, elevator speech makes the networking connection process more effective and less anxiety-prone or stress-inducing. A personal brand is almost like bringing a hype artist or devoted side kick to the party with you.

Networking from Multiple Viewpoints

Think about the last networking event you attended (or party if that is easier). In this scenario it helps to understand two perspectives. By viewing the situation from two vantage points you will maximize your benefits from attending.

The first perspective to consider is that of the event host.

What is the purpose of the event from the perspective of the organization or person planning the event?

One example is a Back-to-School Parent Night. The purpose of the event is to share information about the school, sell spirit wear to raise money for the school, and get parents to volunteer.

Another example is an Insurance Sales Meeting. The purpose of the meeting for the insurance company is to build a sense of community and teach new company wide mandated information to the sales team all at once and in one location.

A third example of networking is through an executive or professional business organization. Professional organizations exist to offer a place to tap into the top people of that field or industry. They also provide a runway of new ideas that make the organization seem to be the industry's answer to local news and the place to be. Depending on who is sponsoring the event or organization, it is also an excellent way to advertise for industry giants.

The second perspective is of that of the attendees, including yourself.

What do you and the other attendees of the networking event hope to gain from attending the event?

Maybe you hope to meet future clients or hire an employee. Perhaps you came to find someone to collaborate or work with. Maybe you hoped to get an edge on the latest trends and technology.

In the Back-to-School example, think about what the parents hope to get out of attending the event. Expecting the teachers to get to know the parents is not the primary reason for the event because the teachers would be completely overwhelmed with remembering the parents of kids they have only spent a few weeks' worth of time teaching. However, a smart parent makes sure to get to know their child's teachers because the next time they may see them one on one will be during report card conferences, which are not always the easiest of meetings.

An added benefit of meeting the teachers is to help provide perspective and humanize each teacher when your child wants to complain about a project, grade, or exam. Humanizing the teacher helps to diffuse the frustrations of the student enough to look for solutions and learn from the experience.

In the second example, the insurance salespersons are looking to catch up with old friends and colleagues, learn who may soon retire and if they can grab their territory or buy their business, and, finally, compare notes on how to best use all the new technology or legal restrictions for their insurance clients.

Finally, in the third example, most of the members attending the organization's lunches or other networking events are there to find clients, get hired, or to fill a requirement by their company or firm to spend time on "networking" or fulfill continuing education requirements for their profession.

The perspectives listed above are all reasonable and authentic. The key to good networking is knowing why you are there, focusing on that goal and being ready to help meet other networkers' goals if you can. The best advice I ever received about networking was simply to be helpful.

Take Time to Celebrate

One of the most wonderful parts of any goal or accomplishment is celebrating it! The act of celebrating encourages continued successful performance. Celebrating inspires us to work harder and mindfully appreciate the moment of accomplishment.

In addition, stopping to celebrate an accomplishment allows for time to consider how to better tackle the next goal or task. By celebrating what went well with one goal, we are better able to prepare for and achieve the next goal.

Take time to celebrate… not just the big achievements but the smaller ones or intermediate ones as well. Celebrate a major milestone on the way to accomplishing an even greater goal. Use the momentum of success to propel you forward to achieve even more.

Take time to celebrate… stepping back and allowing for rest and restoration keeps us primed and ready for the unknown. Celebrating can be a form of self-care by allowing us a break from the continuous list of tasks on our plates. It can include treats, experiences and indulgences that bring us joy, pride, and contentment. Taking time to celebrate also allows for a refilling of our emotional tanks.

Take to time celebrate… to just have fun! Be happy, silly, proud, and emotionally moved by what you have accomplished.

Celebrations do not need to be big or expensive or time-consuming. Create your own list starting with your Joy Creator list from earlier in the book. Add other indulgent and celebratory ideas to create a list of ways to celebrate even the smallest accomplishment. Appreciate your achievements and use that celebration to spur you on to more... but only after stopping to enjoy the moment, mindfully.

Here are some general celebration ideas. Generating your own list of ways to celebrate will be even more motivating.

How to Celebrate

- Call a friend and share your news

- Buy that treat you have been waiting for the right moment to purchase. This could be new shoes, a dessert or meal at your favorite restaurant, sports or technical equipment, a book, ticket to a concert, play or movie, the workout class or coaching session you have been wanting to join. What have you been wishing for and waiting for the right moment of accomplishment to acquire?

- Book a trip for an overnight or weekend away. (See the topic on Planning is More than Half the Fun for why you should book at least a few weeks in advance.)

- Take a mental health afternoon off from work to go to a museum or have a picnic.

- Throw a party (themed or not, big or small, with or without decorations, virtual or in person): Tea, costume, karaoke, beach, online via Facebook Portal or Zoom, etc.

- Book a spa treatment.
- Schedule online gaming with multiple friends for a weeknight for an hour or two.

Celebrate yourself and your accomplishments!

Making the World a Better Place

"You may find that making a difference for others makes the biggest difference in you." – Brian Williams

Boldly, Seth Godin, the author of *This is Marketing*, insists that marketing has evolved to a higher-level form. I completely agree. In fact, the aspects of marketing that I find most appealing are the ability to listen to a person's problem, find a way to solve it, and then communicate with them how they can get that solution. Simple. Kind. Straight forward. A far cry from the advertising and marketing world of the past.

"Better is the change we see when the market embraces what we're offering. Better is what's happening when the culture absorbs our work and improves. Better is when we make the dreams of those we serve come true."
– Seth Godin, This is Marketing.

As I researched more and more for this book, my understanding of what the last part of the book is designed to do expanded beyond just helping you, but also encouraging helping others to make the world a better place.

> *"There is no greater reward than working from your heart and making a difference in the world." – Carlos Santana*

The joy of helping others is well-known and the reward, although not always visible or lucrative, can be immense.

The most important takeaway I got from *This is Marketing* is that we are all capable of making the world a better place through our work and our lives. No matter what our industry or business.

> *"No act of kindness, no matter how small is ever wasted." – Aesop*

In this section, I encourage you to find your own way to make the world a better place. As you carry out your strategic plan, consider how your skills and talents can continue to have an impact on those around you and, in turn, the world as whole. Make that impact great by doing the most you can do with what you have and seeking out ways to make your impact even stronger.

> *"Never doubt that one person can make a difference." – Ingrid Newkirk*

Ask yourself am I making the biggest impact I can in the world? Where can I be a contributor to making the world a better place?

> *"We can change the world and make it a better place. It is in our hands to make a difference." – Nelson Mandela*

How will what I do make the world a more efficient or more amazing place?

> *"Never underestimate the valuable and important difference you make in every life you touch for the impact you make today has a powerful rippling effect on every tomorrow." – Leon Brown*

Chapter 8 Exercises

Pre-Networking Checklist

A quick way to make the time you spend networking worthwhile is to prepare mentally before the event. Take a few minutes to use this pre-networking checklist to prepare for your next event.

- What is your purpose for attending the event?

- Who are the people you hope to meet?

- What help do you need? What is your "ask"?

- What help can you offer to those you meet?

Social Media Checklist for Personal Brands

A weekly social media checklist allows you to prioritize time to focus on your social media without being drawn into the spiral of spending hours reading posts and replying.

Social media can be a huge waste of time if you allow yourself to engage in it for an unlimited amount of time. Plan ahead and create a list of your bare minimum social media weekly tasks to allow you to strategically check social media without being overly distracted. If you have more time to browse, then go ahead and enjoy yourself, knowing you have accomplished the must do list before the fun part.

Weekly List (Only do the tasks for social media platforms you have committed to being engaged in. Ignore the social media platforms you do not want to use.)

Daily Tasks

- Scan the subject line of all work-related emails at the start, middle and end of the workday

- Check notifications for Twitter once per day during the workweek only to respond to direct messages, Retweet posts of interest and thank new followers

Weekly Tasks

- Check, read, and respond to messages or requests to connect on LinkedIn.

- Check Instagram (and/or Pinterest), post one post.

- If a major event occurs or a topic is highly trending, check your schedule and posts to make sure your posts are not seen as insensitive or inappropriate.

Monthly Tasks

- Check and engage with Facebook.

- Set aside 2-4 hours to create posts for all social media platforms to use over the next month.

- Schedule ahead posts for the next 30 days using a scheduler (you may need to do more than once a month depending on the scheduler limitations) or upgrade to an unlimited paid plan to schedule months in advance.

Quarterly Tasks

- Update your customer relationship management software with new connections or new information on current connections.

- Update your content files.

Annual Tasks

- Get a new headshot to update your profile on all social media (If you don't have time or the funds to hire a professional photographer, use your or a friend's phone with a great filter, natural light, and a solid color shirt).

- Review the profile wording or description on all of your social media to keep updated and authentic.

- Set goals for social media and create a plan for number, type, and scheduling of posts for each platform.

- Review your technology needs and equipment, buy new equipment to make managing social media easy.

- Review software to improve or switch to a new software or plan if you have outgrown your current one.

- Consider outsourcing content creation or posting if your budget allows.

Social media is a tool to help us communicate with others. Focusing on the message, the audience, and purpose of each post will help keep the time you spend on social media manageable. Planning what to post and when to post will give you more time for what you are truly passionate about.

Timeline Planner

Part of excellent project management is knowing when to get work done.

One of the best ways to determine when the work will be done is to make a visual plan. By seeing the actual dates to do the work, you are more likely to reach goals.

A Timeline Planner is a productivity tool designed to help plan when projects will actually get accomplished.

This tool works best after you have already completed the Time Map exercise. By having a Time Map of all of the parts of your life, it will be easier to strategically place the different tasks needed to complete your responsibilities and prepare for events that occur throughout the year.

There are many different ways to create a Timeline Planner. Find a method that works for you to get your Timeline Planner completed. Time management or project management software will work. If you prefer a graphical design, try using a graphic design software such as Canva. Use the low tech but equally effective method of writing all of the parts of each project on a 3x5 index cards (or sticky notes) and arrange the cards in order across a timeline of months of the year. Attach to a wall, poster board or take a photo using your phone to print out. Excel spreadsheets or Google Sheets will work as well. Personalize whatever method you choose to work for you. Color coding and using icons can help as well as make the process more fun.

Here is a basic template for a Timeline Planner:

TIME LINE PLANNER

A productivity tool to help plan when projects will actually get accomplished. Use this planner after completing the Time Map exercise to organize how to fulfill commitments, accomplish projects and reach goals this year.

	JANUARY	FEBRUARY	MARCH	APRIL	MAY	JUNE	JULY	AUGUST	SEPTEMBER	OCTOBER	NOVEMBER	DECEMBER
FAMILY				Spring Break				Vacation				Winter Break
WORK: MAIN			Q1 Report			Q2 Report			Q3 Report			Q4 Report
WORK: PROJECT A		New Product Launch					Product Annual Review				Choose new product line	
WORK: TEAM				Prepare for Annual Meeting	Annual Meeting Team Retreat		Strategy Planning					Team Review
SELF CARE								Monthly Meeting with Personal Trainer and Nutritionist				
FRIENDS						College Friend Weekend						Holiday Party
VOLUNTEERING			Fundraising Gala								Fall 5K fundraiser	
CAREER		Update Resume Personal Brand				Industry Conference		New Head Shots		Alumni Event		
SIDE HUSTLE					Due Diligence				Loan Application		Finalize website	Content Calendar

213

Conclusion

Congratulations! By completing the exercises in this book and contemplating the various topics discussed throughout, you have worked hard to better understand how to find fun and fulfillment in your life and career.

After reading and doing the exercises in this book, I encourage you to act to reach your goals and to embrace your unique personal brand. Follow the plan you developed to find the best opportunities out there for you. I wish you continued energy, motivation, and inspiration.

Revisit and redo the exercises at critical moments in your journey, remembering that we are all a work in progress, myself included. Please reach out to me via my Twitter handle @creativebrandch to share comments, new concepts, and make suggestions about or discuss topics from this book.

As you continue your personal brand journey remember these two things: One, be true to your own authentic personal brand. Two, try to make the world a better place by helping others.

Life is too fragile and short to not live it to the fullest. Why not do so in a way that makes it fulfilling!

I hope every day brings you more fun and fulfillment!

Acknowledgements

This book would not exist without a lot of help from God and many, many kind friends.

Thank you to David J.P. Fisher, Katherine Don, Liz Yablonicky, Rozan Norris, Cari Smith, Carolyn Barth, Jen Schuman and Amy Boyle for support, wisdom, and encouragement over and above my expectations.

Thank you to the many friends and colleagues that inspired and discussed the concepts in this book, listened patiently, tested out exercises and helped me with research: Anne Linnen, Katie Baal, Nicole Price, Marla Price Krantz, Kara Kuo, Jim Mullen, Ashley Koenigsknecht, Ian Carswell, Viva Bartkus, Aideen Shea, Alice Sisbarro, Mark J. Carter, Jen Pacourek, Kristen Smith, Joe and Joan Jablonski, Larry Yablonicky, Becky Christie, Troy Sandidge, Alissa Spera, Anna Bax, Stephanie Gordon, Lori Benvenuto, Tiffany Bernard, Randy Hlavac, Andy Crestodina, Kristen Palana, Daleele Allison and Vicky Shanta Retelny.

Thank you to my dear family from coast to coast, the Selling Launchpad Group, and the lovely people that make the Foundation for Hearing and Speech Rehabilitation, National Speakers Association-Illinois and Friends of Payton run so smoothly!

To my kids and my own personal backer, hype man, investor, muse, editor, best friend, super dad to my kids and awesome husband...Thank you for putting up with my frantic attempts to find time to write and endless questions. Please know none of this would be possible without you.

Notes

Part One
Discovering and Building your Personal Brand

Newman, Randy. Performed by Jenifer Lewis featuring the Pinnacle Gospel Choir and Anika Noni Rose *(2009)*. *Dig a Little Deeper*. On ***The Princess and the Frog: Original Songs and Score*** California: Walt Disney Records.

Chapter 1
Personal Branding Basics: What is Personal Branding?

Condren, Erin. "7 Hidden Benefits of Planning", *Thrive Global*. 1 February 2020. https://thriveglobal.com/stories/7-hidden-benefits-of-planning/

Mulligan, Amanda. "Survey Says: Vacation Planning Leads to Greater Happiness", *Travelzoo*. 25 January 2018. https://www.travelzoo.com/blog/survey-says-vacation-planning-leads-greater-happiness/

Daly, Annie. "Trip Planning Is Basically My Therapy—Here's How I Make Travel Happen No Matter What", *SELF*. 16 January 2018. https://www.self.com/story/tri p-planning-is-basically-my-therapy-heres-how-i-make-travel-happen-no-matter-what

Nawijin, Jeroen, Marchand, Miquelle A., Veenhoven, Ruut and Vingerhoets, Ad J.. "Vacationers Happy, But Most not Happier After a Holiday", *Applied Research in Quality of Life*. 10 February 2010.

https://link.springer.com/article/10.1007%2Fs11482-009-9091-9

Rosenbloom, Stephanie. "What a Great Trip! And I'm Not Even There Yet", *The New York Times*. 7 May 2014. https://www.nytimes.com/2014/05/11/travel/what-a-great-trip-and-im-not-even-there-yet.html

Michael, MA, Raphailia. "What Self-Care Is – and What It Isn't", *Psych Central*. 8 July 2018. https://psychcentral.com/blog/what-self-care-is-and-what-it-isnt-2/

Baratta, Maria. "Self-Care 101: 10 Ways to Take Better Care of You", *Psychology Today*. 27 May 2018. https://www.psychologytoday.com/us/blog/skinny-revisited/201805/self-care-101

Scott, S.J.. "275 Self-Care Ideas & Activities to Deal with Life (2020)", *Develop Good Habits*. 2020. https://www.developgoodhabits.com/self-care-ideas/

Stillman, Jessica. "Never Been Able to Keep a Journal Before? This is a Journal Format for You.", *Inc.* 5 December 2017. https://www.inc.com/jessica-stillman/never-been-able-to-keep-a-journal-before-this-is-journal-format-for-you.html

Johnson, M.D., Spencer, *Out of the Maze* (New York, New York: Portfolio/Penguin Putnam, 2018).

Johnson, M.D., Spencer, *Who Moved My Cheese?* (New York, New York: G.P. Putnam's Sons, 2002).

Chapter 2
Authenticity: Get to know who you are at your core

Frei, Frances and Morriss, Anne. *Unleashed: The Unapologetic Leader's Guide to Empowering Everyone Around You* (New York: Harvard Business Review Press (2 June 2020).

Schulte, Brigid. *Overwhelmed Work, Love, and Play When No One has the Time* (New York: Sarah Crichton Books/Farra, Straus and Giroux, 2014).

Csikszentmihalyi, Mihaly. *Flow: The Psychology of Optimal Experience* (New York: HarperCollins, 2008).

Raffone, A., Srinivasan, N. Mindfulness and Cognitive Functions: Toward a Unifying Neurocognitive Framework. *Mindfulness*. 2017. https://doi.org/10.1007/s12671-016-0654-1

Dufu, Tiffany, *Drop the Ball.*(New York: Flatiron Books, 2017).

McKeown, Greg, *Essentialism: The Disciplined Pursuit of Less.* (New York: Crown Business, 2014).

Dweck, Ph.D., Carol S., *Mindset* (New York: Random House, 2006).

Pride. (2020). Dictionary.com. Retrieved from https://www.dictionary.com/browse/pride?s=t

Talent. (2020). Workable.com. Retrieved from https://resources.workable.com/hr-terms/talent-definition

Skills (2020) Merriam-Webster. Retrieved from
https://www.merriam-webster.com/dictionary/skills

Chapter 3
Find your Inspiration: Look back to move forward

Tan, Chade-Meng, *Search Inside Yourself: The Unexpected Path to Achieving Success, Happiness*, (New York: HarperCollins, 2012).

DiNardi, Gaetano, "Why you should work less and spend more time on hobbies". *Harvard Business Review*. 7 February 2019. https://hbr.org/2019/02/why-you-should-work-less-and-spend-more-time-on-hobbies?fbclid=IwAR2W-pDkKLJeh-HJOjAuhMEfJpx_EQB--5k5DBPnaqPBGe0_j1O6QCNb0IU

Kaimal, G., Carroll-Haskins, K. Berberian, M.G., Dougherty, A. Carlton, N.R. & Ramakrishnan, A., "Changes in Measures of Stress Affect, Anxiety, self-efficacy, and Salivary Biomarkers as a Result of Therapeutic Artmaking in Patients Undergoing Radiation Oncology Treatment: A Mixed Methods Pilot Study. *Integrative Cancer Therapies*. 2020.

Anderson-Lopez, Kristen, Lopez, Robert. Performed by Idina Menzel. *(2014). Let it Go.* On *Frozen: Original Songs and Score* California: Walt Disney Records.

Tan, Chade-Meng, Search Inside Yourself: The Unexpected Path to Achieving Success, Happiness (New York: HarperCollins, 2012).

Roth, Eric, *The Curious Case of Benjamin Button.* Screenplay, 2008.

Chapter 4
Discover what you love to do: Finding your favorite
work and life activities

Rubin, Gretchen, *The Happiness Project: or Why I Spent a Year Trying to Sing in the Morning, Clean My Closets, Fight Right, Read Aristotle and Generally Have More Fun.*(New York, New York: HarperCollins Publishers, 2018).

Rubin, Gretchen, "Happier". https://gretchenrubin.com/podcasts/

McKeown, Greg, *Essentialism: The Disciplined Pursuit of Less.* (New York: Crown Business, 2014).

Bennett, Heather H. *Small Business, Big Brand.* 2019. https://brandmarketing.home.blog/

Duhigg, Charles, The Power of Habit (New York, New York: Random House, 2012).

Retelny, RDN, LDN, Victoria Shanta, *Total Body Diet for Dummies* (Hoboken, New Jersey: John Wiley & Sons, Inc, 2016).

Tremayne, Dr. Kell, Hannagan, Kimberley, "Franklin Covey System – Is it Right for You?", *My Time Management.* 2016. http://www.mytimemanagement.com/franklin-covey.html

Jager, Chris, "11 Ways to Improve Productivity without Coffee", *Lifehacker.* 6 March 2019. https://www.lifehacker.com.au/2019/03/11-ways-to-improve-productivity-without-coffee-infographic/

Chapter 5
Create your Future: Dare to Dream

Kaufman, Scott Barry, "The Need for Pretend Play in Child Development". *Psychology Today*. 6 March 2012. https://www.psychologytoday.com/us/blog/beautiful-minds/201203/the-need-pretend-play-in-child-development

McMeekin, Gail, *The 12 Secrets of Highly Creative Women: A Portable Mentor* (Conari Press; Later Printing Edition, 2000).
Passion. (2020). Dictionary.com. Retrieved from https://www.dictionary.com/
Strengths. (2020). Dictionary.com. Retrieved from https://www.vocabulary.com/dictionary/strengths

The Muse Editor, "How to Think Like a Creative Every Day". *The Muse*. 2020. https://www.themuse.com/advice/how-to-think-like-a-creative-every-day

Colorit Support, "7 Benefits of Coloring for Adults and Why You Should Join the Adult Coloring Craze", *Colorit Blog*. 5 February 2016. https://www.colorit.com/blogs/news/85320388-amazing-benefits-of-coloring-for-adults

Passion (2020) Lexico. Retrieved from https://www.lexico.com/en/definition/passion

Strengths (2020) The Free Dictionary. Retrieved from https://www.thefreedictionary.com/Strengths

McLeod, Saul, "Maslow's Hierarchy of Needs", *Simply Psychology*. 20 March 2020. https://www.simplypsychology.org/maslow.html

Yarrow, Kit, Ph.D., "Back-to-School Shopping: It Goes Deeper Than You Think", *Psychology Today*. 14 August 2018. https://www.psychologytoday.com/us/blog/the-why-behind-the-buy/201808/back-school-shopping-it-goes-deeper-you-think

Rampton, John, "10 Ways to Create a More Productive Work Environment", *Entrepreneur*. 9 July 2019. https://www.entrepreneur.com/article/336044

Chapter 6
Find your place: Seek where you are needed in the world

Bennett, Heather H. "Target Marketing 101", *Small Business, Big Brand*. May 2019. https://brandmarketing.home.blog/2019/05/01/target-marketing-101/

Chapter 7
Creating your Strategic Personal Brand Plan: specific tasks and actions to achieve your ideal work and life

Whilliams, A. V,,"Time for Happiness: Why the Pursuit of Money Isn't Bringing You Joy and What Will", *Harvard Business Review*. 29 January 2019.

Nichols, Wallace J., *Blue Mind* (New York, New York: Little, Brown and Company, 2014).

Wang, Y., Jones, B.F. & Wang, D. "Early-career setback and future career impact". *Nature Communications*. (1 October 2019). https://www.nature.com/articles/s41467-019-12189-3

Denney, J.D., Williams, P. *The Success Intersection: What Happens when your Talent Meets Your Passion.* (Grand Rapids, Michigan, 2017).

Busch, Christian, *The Serendipity Mindset.* (New York: Riverhead Books, 2020).

Busch, Christian. "How to Create Your Own Career Luck". *Harvard Business Review.* 24 August 2020. https://hbr-org.cdn.ampproject.org/c/s/hbr.org/amp/2020/08/how-to-create-your-own-career-luck

Facebook. (2020). Webwise. Retrieved from https://www.webwise.ie/parents/explained-what-is-facebook-2/

Egan, Karisa, "The Difference Between Facebook, Twitter, LinkedIn, YouTube &
Pinterest [Updated for 2020]", *Impact.* 10 February 2017. https://www.impactbnd.com/blog/the-difference-between-facebook-twitter-linkedin-google-youtube-pinterest

Twitter. (2020). *Hubspot.* Retrieved from https://blog.hubspot.com/marketing/what-is-twitter

Instagram. (2020), *Pocket-lint.* Retrieved from https://www.pocket-lint.com/apps/news/instagram/133957-how-instagram-works-plus-tips-and-tricks

Elliot, Ben. "Instagram and Its Benefits". *Social We Talk.* 13 January 2016.
https://www.socialwetalk.com/blog/2016/1/13/instagram-and-its-benefits

Gotter, Ana. "Pinterest vs. Instagram: How to Use Both to Boost Your Business". *Ad Espresso*. 24 October 2017. https://adespresso.com/blog/pinterest-vs-instagram/

LinkedIn. (2020). *Business Insider*. Retrieved from https://www.businessinsider.com/what-is-linkedin

Blog. (2020). First Site Guide. Retrieved from https://firstsiteguide.com/what-is-blog/

Bennett, Heather H. "Brand Plans for Bloggers", *Small Business, Big Brand*. June 2019. https://brandmarketing.home.blog/2019/06/05/brand-plans-for-bloggers/

Websites. (2020) *The Orbit Media Blog*. https://www.orbitmedia.com/blog-start-here/ Recommendation: spend time reading this blog for the best tips for website. Too many excellent blog posts to list.

Chapter 8
Keeping your Personal Brand Strong: checkups, maintenance and updates

Fisher, David J.P., *Networking in the 21st Century,* (Chicago: Rockstar Publishing, 2015).

Godin, Seth, *This is Marketing* (New York, New York: Portfolio/Penguin, 2018).

Scott, S.J. "Morning Routine Habits (2020)", *Develop Good Habits*. 2020. https://www.developgoodhabits.com/morning-routine-habits/

Schulte, Brigid. *Overwhelmed Work, Love, and Play When No One has the Time* (New York: Sarah Crichton Books/Farra, Straus and Giroux, 2014).

Williams, Ashley, "Time for Happiness, Why the Pursuit of Money Isn't Bringing you Joy and What Will". *Harvard Business Review*. 24 January 2019.https://hbr.org/cover-story/2019/01/time-for-happiness

AJR (2019). 100 Bad Days. On *Neotheater* [single] New York: BMG.

Denney, J.D., Williams, P. *The Success Intersection: What Happens when your Talent Meets Your Passion*. (Grand Rapids, Michigan, 2017).

Busch, Christian, *The Serendipity Mindset*. (New York: Riverhead Books, 2020).

Quotations

Authenticity

"You've got to dig a little deeper." – Mama Odie of <u>The Princess and the Frog</u>

"Find out what you like doing best and get someone to pay you for it." – Katharine Whitehorn

"If you don't love what you do, you won't do it with much conviction or passion." – Mia Hamm

"Ever since I was a child, I have had this instinctive urge for expansion and growth. To me, the function and duty of a quality human being is the sincere and honest development of one's potential." – Bruce Lee

"One of the most courageous things you can do is identify yourself, know who you are, what you believe in and where you want to go." – Sheila Murray Bethel

 "It is never too late to be what you might have been." – George Eliot

"Love yourself enough to create an environment in your life that is conducive to the nourishment of your personal growth." – Steve Maraboli

"When your greatest talent intersects with your greatest passion, you have discovered your sweet spot in life." – James D. Denney and Pat Williams

"With a serendipity mindset, every interaction might open a new path — for finding love, meeting an investor, making a friend, forging a new interest, or landing a new job."
– Christian Busch

"Authenticity is a collection of choices that we have to make every day. It's about the choice to show up and be real. The choice to be honest. The choice to let out true selves be seen." – Brene Brown

"I think self-awareness is probably the most important thing toward being a champion."
– Billie Jean King

"When we're growing up there are all sorts of people telling us what to do
when really what we need is space to work out who to be." – Elliot Page

"Authenticity, logic, and empathy are the most vital skills an employee can have."
– Frances Frei

"It takes courage to grow up and become who you really are." – E.E. Cummings

Motivation

"Flood your life with ideas from many sources. Creativity needs to be exercised like a muscle." – Brian Tracy

"Don't let perfectionism become an excuse for never getting started." – Marilu Henner

"If you don't like the road you're walking, pave another one." – Dolly Parton

"Step out of the history that is holding you back. Step into the new story you are willing to create." – Oprah Winfrey

"It is not in the stars to hold our destiny, but in ourselves." – William Shakespeare

"Don't wait until everything is just right. It will never be perfect. There will always be challenges, obstacles, and less than perfect conditions. So what? Get started now. With each step you take, you will grow stronger and stronger, more and more skilled, more and more self-confident, and more and more successful." – Mark Victor Hansen

"The only impossible journey is the one you never begin."– Tony Robbins

"I choose to make the rest of my life the best of my life." – Louise Hay

"You are allowed to be both a masterpiece & a work in progress simultaneously." – Sophia Bush

"Destiny is no matter of chance. It is a matter of choice. It is not a thing to be waited for, it is a thing to be achieved." – William Jennings Bryan

"Change your life today. Don't gamble on the future, act now, without delay." – Simone de Beauvoir

"Efforts and courage are not enough without purpose and direction." – John F. Kennedy

"Do not wait; the time will never be 'just right.' Start where you stand, and work with whatever tools you may have at your command, and better tools will be found as you go along." – George Herbert.

"If you don't like the road you're walking, pave another one." – Dolly Parton

"Step out of the history that is holding you back. Step into the new story you are willing to create." – Oprah Winfrey

"It is not in the stars to hold our destiny, but in ourselves." – William Shakespeare

Success

"I've learned that making a living is not the same thing as making a life." - Maya Angelou

"What I know is, is that if you do work that you love, and the work fulfills you, the rest will come." – Oprah Winfrey

"Everyone has a purpose in life and a unique talent to give to others. And when we blend this unique talent with service to others, we experience the ecstasy and exultation of our

spirit, which is the ultimate goal of all goals."
– Kallam Anji Reddy

"If you want to discover the true character of a person, you have only to observe what they are passionate about." – Shannon L. Alder

"Working hard for something we don't care about is called stressed; working hard for something we love is called passion."
– Simon Sinek

"The secret of joy in work is contained in one word – excellence. To know how to do something well is to enjoy it." – Pearl Buck

Believe in yourself

"We must have perseverance and, above all, confidence in ourselves. We must believe we are gifted for something and that this thing must be attained." – Marie Curie

"Don't wait until you reach your goal to be proud of yourself. Be proud of every step you take." – Karen Salmansohn

"There are no great limits to growth because there are no limits of human intelligence, imagination, and wonder." – Ronald Reagan

"I can't change the direction of the wind, but I can adjust my sails to always reach my destination." – Jimmy Dean

"What you put into life is what you get out of it." – Clint Eastwood

"If your dreams do not scare you, they are not big enough." – Ellen Johnson Sirleaf

"Growth is never by mere chance; it is the result of forces working together." – James Cash Penney

"Big dreams create the magic that stir men's souls to greatness." – Bill McCartney

"You are never too old to set another goal or to dream a new dream."
– C.S. Lewis

"Keep your dreams alive. Understand to achieve anything requires faith and belief in yourself, vision, hard work, determination, and dedication. Remember all things are possible for those who believe." – Gail Devers

"All our dreams come true, if we have the courage to pursue them." – Walt Disney

"There is no substitute for persistence. The person who makes persistence his watchword, discovers that "Old Man Failure" finally becomes tired, and makes his departure. Failure cannot cope with persistence." – Napoleon Hill.

"Success is liking yourself, liking what you do, and liking how you do it." – Maya Angelou

"You learn in life that the only person you can really correct, and change is yourself."
– Katharine Hepburn

"If you write something down on paper, it becomes an actual goal.   Before you write it down, it's a thought, a dream that may or may not get done." – Summer Sanders

"To achieve great things, we must not only act, but also dream. Not only plan but also believe." – Anatole France

Hope

"Between stimulus and response there is a space. In that space is our power to choose our response. In our response lies our growth and our freedom." – Viktor E. Frankl

"Hope does not disappoint." – Romans 5:5.

"'I don't think things ever go back to how they were. Here's my thought, though: maybe they can turn out better than they were." – Hope of <u>Out of the Maze</u>

"Optimism is the faith that leads to achievement. Nothing can be done without hope and confidence." – Helen Keller

Self-Care

"Actively planning, instead of passively reacting, is proven to reduce stress and can lead to more fulfilling, intentional living."
– Erin Condren

"Self-care is any activity that we do deliberately in order to take care of our mental, emotional, and physical health."
– Raphailia Michael, MA.

"Almost everything will work again if you unplug it for a few minutes, including you."
– Anne Lamott

"Needs lower down in the hierarchy must be satisfied before individuals can attend to needs higher up." – Saul McLeod

"Don't be too hard on yourself. There are plenty of people willing to do that for you."
– Susan Gale.

"Mindfulness allows you to develop a broad set of cognitive and executive functions, raises self-awareness levels and facilitate emotional regulation, empowering individuals to substitute knee-jerk reactions with more conscious and ultimately more efficient behavior." – Raffone, A., Srinivasan, N.

"Those who think they have not time for bodily exercise will sooner or later have to find time for illness." – Edward Stanley

"It's the heightened state of being that lets whatever you're doing be your best life, from moment to astonishing moment." – Oprah Winfrey

"Being on, in, and near water can be among the most cost-effective ways of reducing stress and anxiety." – Wallace J. Nichols

Personal Branding, Business and Marketing

"We all have personal brands and most of us have already left a digital footprint, whether we like it or not. Proper social media use highlights your strengths that may not shine through in an interview or application and gives the world a broader view of who you are. Use it wisely." – Amy Jo Martin, Celebrity Brand Strategist to Shaquille O'Neal, Dana White (UFC) & Dwayne "The Rock" Johnson

"Target Marketing means you are putting your customer and their needs at the center of your focus and attention. You are making your customer the most important aspect of doing business, so your products/services are the best they can be. " – Heather H. Bennett

Happiness

"You are the one that possesses the keys to your being. You carry the passport to your own happiness." – Diane von Furstenberg

"It's statistically proven that time spent planning vacation directly correlates with greater happiness in your personal and professional lives." – Amanda Mulligan

"When you're traveling, you're forced to deal with new experiences and stimuli at a faster pace, which means that, if you handle them well, you may end up experiencing more 'small feelings of success' than you do at home" – Annie Daly

"Those successes are so rewarding that many people return from trips feeling a lot better about themselves, like they've achieved—which leads to higher self-esteem overall." – Michael Brein, Ph.D.,

"The practical lesson for an individual is that you derive most of your happiness from anticipating the holiday trip." – Jeroen Nawijn

"Turns out, there is an art to anticipation. Savoring is an active, not passive, process." – Elizabeth Dunn

Strength

"It's the friends that you can call up at 4 a.m. that matter." – Marlene Dietrich

"What doesn't kill you makes you stronger." – Kelly Clarkson

"That which does not kill us, makes us stronger." – Nietzsche

"Choose to focus your time, energy and conversation around people who inspire you, support you and help you to grow you into your happiest, strongest, wisest self." – Karen Salmansohn

"When you seek advice, do not withhold facts from the person whose advice you seek."
– Abu Baker

"Seek out a personal coach or mentor in the workplace. He/she should push you when you need it by encouraging and motivating you. Don't be afraid of their honesty." – Cathy Engelbert

"But failure has to be an option in art and in exploration--because it's a leap of faith. And no important endeavor that required innovation was done without risk. You have to be willing to take those risks." – James Cameron

"A hundred bad days made a hundred good stories
A hundred good stories make me interesting at parties
Yeah, no, I ain't scared of you
No, I ain't scared of you no more" – AJR

"I've failed over and over and over again in my life and that is why I succeed. "– Michael Jordan

Fun

"When people don't have time for hobbies, businesses pay a price. Hobbies can make

workers substantially better at their jobs."
– Gaetano DiNardi

"When you recover or discover something that nourishes your soul and brings joy, care enough about yourself to make room for it in your life." – Jean Shinoda Bolen

"just about 45 minutes of free art-making in a studio attended by an art therapist was enough to increase a person's self-efficacy — a term used to describe a person's confidence in themselves and their ability to complete tasks." – Girija Kaimail, EdD

"When you recover or discover something that nourishes your soul and brings joy, care enough about yourself to make room for it in your life." – Jean Shinoda Bolen

"If you obey all the rules, you miss all the fun." – Katharine Hepburn

Time

"Sorry I'm late. I got here as soon as I wanted to." – Karen Walker of Will & Grace

"Time is a created thing. To say, 'I don't have time,' is like saying, 'I don't want to.'" – Lao Tzu

"You may delay, but time will ot." – Benjamin Franklin

"Those who make the worst use of their time are the first to complain of its brevity." – Jean de La Bruyère

"Those who think they have not time for bodily exercise will sooner or later have to find time for illness." – Edward Stanley

"You can have it all. Just not all at once." – Oprah Winfrey

Moving on

"Let it go!" – Elsa of <u>Frozen</u>

"The key is to let go of two things: grasping and aversion. Grasping is when the mind desperately holds on to something and refuses to let it go. Aversion is when the mind desperately keeps something away and refuses to let it come. These two qualities are flip sides of each other. Grasping and aversion together account for a huge percentage of the suffering we experience, perhaps 90 percent, maybe even 100 percent." – Chade-Meng Tan

"And now that you don't have to be perfect, you can be good." – John Steinbeck

"When things are a disappointment, try not to be so discouraged." – Carol Burnett

"For what it's worth: it's never too late or, in my case, too early to be whoever you want to be. There's no time limit, stop whenever you want. You can change or stay the same, there are no rules to this thing. We can make the best or the worst of it. I hope you make the best of it. And I hope you see things that startle you. I hope you feel things you never felt before. I hope you meet people with a different point of view. I hope you live a life you're proud of. If you find that you're not, I hope you have the courage to start all over again." – Eric Roth

Make the World a Better Place

"No act of kindness, no matter how small is ever wasted." – Aesop.

"Compassion for others begins with kindness to ourselves." – Pema Chondron

"If you have a sense of your place in the world, that's the best preparation for anything." – Casey Wilson

"Work gives you meaning, and purpose and life is empty without it." – Stephen Hawking

"You may find that making a difference for others makes the biggest difference in you." – Brian Williams

"Better is the change we see when the market embraces what we're offering. Better is what happening when the culture absorbs our work and improves. Better is when we make the dreams of those, we serve come true." – Seth Godin

"There is no greater reward than working from your heart and making a difference in the world." – Carlos Santana

"Never doubt that one person can make a difference." – Ingrid Newkirk

"Never underestimate the valuable and important difference you make in every life you touch for the impact you make today has a powerful rippling effect on every tomorrow." – Leon Brown

"Success means we go to sleep at night knowing that our talents and abilities were used in a way that served others." – Marianne Williamson

"We can change the world and make it a better place. It is in our hands to make a difference." – Nelson Mandela

"Every great dream begins with a dreamer. Always remember, you have within you the strength, the patience, and the passion to reach for the stars to change the world." – Harriet Tubman

Index

About the Author

Heather H. Bennett is a marketing strategist and personal brand coach with 20+ years of experience, including marketing brands such as VO5, Vaseline, Ponds, Pyrex, and Claussen Pickles. Drawing from her MBA and Social Media Marketing Certification, she coaches her clients to create strong, authentic, and unique brands through her business, Creative Brand Coach.

Working jobs as varied as assembly line worker, national chain restaurant host, research biologist, brand manager, small business owner, and board of directors' member has shaped Heather's unique perspective on personal branding and careers. Her personal branding method has been shared at workshops and webinars through her workbook, *Personal Branding for Fulfillment in Life, Work & Play*.

Heather lives in Chicago, Illinois with her husband and four children, where she enjoys volunteering for non-profits, reading mystery novels and spending as much time as possible outside swimming, kayaking, and hiking.

To connect with Heather about marketing, social media, and personal branding, visit her website:

www.creativebrandcoach.net

Made in the USA
Coppell, TX
08 December 2020

43791758R00144